Past-into-Present series

LAW AND ORDER

Brian Ashley

Assistant Master, Marlborough College

B. T. BATSFORD LTD LONDON

First Published 1967
© Brian Ashley, 1967

Printed in Great Britain by William Clowes and Sons, Ltd,
London and Beccles and bound by Dorstel Press Ltd, Harlow, Essex
for the Publishers
B. T. Batsford Ltd, 4 Fitzhardinge Street, London W1

Acknowledgment

The author and publishers wish to thank the following for the illustrations appearing in this book: the Bodleian Library, Oxford for fig. 14; the Trustees of the British Museum for figs. 1, 30 and 34; the Central Office of Information (Crown Copyright reserved) for figs. 56 and 57; Central Press Photos Ltd for fig. 61; the Commissioner of Police, New Scotland Yard for fig. 58; the Mansell Collection for figs. 3, 13, 15, 16, 21, 25, 29, 32, 35, 40, 41, 44, 46, 47, 48, 49, 51, 52 and 53; the Press Association for figs. 55 and 59; the *Radio Times* Hulton Picture Library for figs. 4, 6, 18, 22, 24, 37, 38, 39 and 50; the Topical Press Agency Ltd for fig. 54; the Master and Fellows of Trinity College, Cambridge for fig. 2; St Marylebone Public Library for fig. 33; the Society of Friends for fig. 43. The diagrams on p. 93 are reproduced by courtesy of Her Majesty's Stationery Office (Crown Copyright reserved).

The author's thanks are also due to Colin Davies and Dr P. N. Carter, heads of the history departments at Charterhouse and Marlborough College, for their helpful suggestions, and to his colleague John Osborne for reading the proofs.

Contents

Acknowledgment 2

List of Illustrations 4

LAW AND FREEDOM 5

1 FROM ANGLO-SAXON TIMES
   TO THE END OF THE MIDDLE
   AGES 7
   Kinship 8
   Mutual Responsibility 9
   The Influence of the Normans 9
   Henry II's Achievements,
      1154–89 10
   Magna Carta, 1215 11
   Edward I's Statute of Win-
      chester, 1285 11
   Justices of the Peace and Con-
      stables 12
   Methods of Trial 12
   Medieval Punishments 14
   The End of the Middle Ages 16

2 THE TUDOR AND STUART
   PERIODS 1485–1688 19
   Local Government and Justices
      of the Peace 20
   The Duties of the Justices 20
   Punishments 22
   The Poor and Vagrancy 23
   Cromwellian Rule and the
      Legacy of Hatred of Strong
      Government 26

3 EIGHTEENTH CENTURY—'OUT
   OF ORDER' 30
   Population Increase and Grow-
      ing Urbanisation 30
   The Effects of Enclosure 31
   City Life 32
   London 33

Gin Drinking 34
Parish Constables 34
Jonathan Wild 37
The Secretary of State 38

4 MAKERS OF THE POLICE—THE
   FORE-RUNNERS 41
   Henry Fielding 41
   Patrick Colquhoun 46
   'Charlies' 47
   Parliamentary Concern 48

5 PEEL AND THE REFORM OF THE
   PENAL CODE 50
   Social Distress and Rioting 50
   The Luddites 51
   The Peace-keeping System 53
   'Massacre of Peterloo' 55
   Sir Robert Peel 56
   The Metropolitan Police Force 59

6 PRISONS AND HANGINGS 62
   Prison Reformers 64
   John Howard 64
   Elizabeth Fry 65
   Transportation 69
   Improvements to the Penal
      System 71

7 VICTORIAN ERA—APPLE-PIE
   ORDER 74
   Chartism 76
   The Extension of the Police
      System 78

8 THE PRESENT AND THE FUTURE? 84
   Causes of Crime 86
   Number of Crimes 87
   The Remedies? 89
   Punishment 90
   End of Capital Punishment? 90

The Illustrations

1 The King's Court or Witan 7
2 Administration of justice, thirteenth century 9
3 Taking the oath 11
4 Trial by ordeal 13
5 Men in prison and the stocks, twelfth century 14
6 A baker drawn to the pillory 15
7 Death by burning 16
8 A public execution, fourteenth century 17
9 The burning of Anne Askew and Jacels, 1546 21
10 The Elizabethan Underworld 22
11 Whipping and beating a vagabond 23
12 The stocks in Tudor England 24
13 Court of Wards and Liveries in the reign of Elizabeth 25
14 Martyrdom of Catholic Priests 26
15 The water torture 27
16 The Watchman or Bellman of London, 1616 28
17 The 'penitent murtherer', late seventeenth century 29
18 The ducking punishment, eighteenth century 31
19 A London street brawl 33
20 'Gin Lane' as seen by Hogarth 35
21 A Charlie or watchman, eighteenth century 36
22 Jonathan Wild on his way to Tyburn, 1725 38
23 An execution outside Newgate Prison 39
24 Henry Fielding 41
25 Townshend, the Bow Street Runner 42
26 John Wilkes 43
27 The Gordon Riots, 1780 45
28 Prisoners on the way to execution 47
29 The pillory, 1808 48
30 A poacher before the magistrate 51
31 Jeremiah Brandeth, the Nottingham Captain 52
32 The 'Massacre of Peterloo', 1819 54
33 The Cato Street Conspiracy, 1820 55
34 Duelling, nineteenth century 56
35 The burning of Bristol, 1831 57
36 Regency 'Bucks' and the Charlies 58
37 Sir Robert Peel, 1788–1850 59
38 Peelers in Bow Street, late 1830's 60
39 A transport ship, nineteenth century 63
40 Chain gang, 1831 65
41 Prison ship at Portsmouth, 1828 66
42 Flogging at Newgate Prison, nineteenth century 67
43 Elizabeth Fry at Newgate, 1823 68
44 A nineteenth century execution 69
45 Plan of Pentonville Prison, 1845 70
46 Inside Brixton Prison, nineteenth century 71
47 Debtor in the Fleet Prison 72
48 Chartist Riots at Newport, 1839 77
49 A Peeler, 1837–8 79
50 Tom Smith, a well-known London policeman 79
51 The Police wear beards—cartoon 80
52 'Specials' receiving instruction, 1887 81
53 The Siege of Sydney Street, 1911 82
54 Suffragettes being taken into custody 83
55 Police controlling crowds, 1966 85
56 Policewoman using two-way radio 87
57 The Identikit in use 88
58 A police-dog in action 91
59 Sewing mail bags in Durham Prison 92
60 Indictable offences, 1938–65 93
61 A cell in Wormwood Scrubs 94

Law and Freedom

Over two thousand years ago, Aristotle, the famous Greek philosopher said: 'Man is a political animal.' He meant by this that man is naturally gregarious and enjoys living with others in an orderly society. He was talking of men participating in the kind of advanced civilisation which prevailed in the Greek city states of his time, such as Athens—but his dictum is true of the history of mankind.

From earliest times the benefits of communal life have been easily discernible; indeed, it is difficult to think of man existing outside some form of society. Whether man is part of an advanced, urban civilisation, or a member of a primitive, even nomadic, tribe, he obtains such benefits as security, companionship and a more ordered existence. These he would miss if he were to fend for himself.

One thing all these associations of people have in common is that men have found it necessary to impose certain rules and regulations upon the members who make up the community. Perhaps the most important heritage of the Roman civilisation is their system of law, much of which has been assimilated into the modern world. Other communities have, however, established some form of law and order without such an advanced body of written law produced: tribal customs and laws, handed down by word of mouth, even in the most primitive of societies regulate the conduct of both family and communal life.

Today we accept, though not always without question, the presence of rules and regulations in the smaller associations to which we belong—the family, the school or youth club. In our everyday behaviour we obey, subconsciously for the most part, rules such as having decent or civilised manners which do not cause offence to others. Many other rules, though, are written down and embodied in law and are disobeyed only under penalty of punishment. If people were not governed in their daily behaviour by certain customs, taboos and enforceable laws, then society as such could easily degenerate into chaos and anarchy. The Highway Code is a set of rules organised to ensure the safety and mobility of road users. If drivers universally ignored their code, traffic would be in confusion and a danger to all. Although individuals have to give up some measure of their freedom and independence when they accept laws, they realise that this sacrifice is for the good of the community as a whole—and hence for their own further good.

The kind of situation which could arise in a community suddenly placed outside the restraining and guiding influence of law is very well described by William Golding in his novel *Lord of the Flies*. A community of boys stranded on an island gradually degenerates so that well-behaved choir boys turn into a gang of violent savages.

English Law can be divided into two main sections: Criminal Law, which deals largely with offences for which people can be punished, and Civil Law, which concerns disputes between two or more people and which usually has nothing to do with the question of punishment. Both sections fall within the sphere of what is called Common Law. This has slowly grown out of the decisions made by judges from earliest times. When reaching a decision judges often took into account the local customs and unwritten rules of their times; when written down, these decisions became accepted laws until they were altered to meet new circumstances. Some of the ancient Common Law is written into Acts of Parliament but much remains unwritten.

Statute Law is different in that it is written and laid down by the authority of Parliament and has to be followed by the judges exactly as it is written—the Factory, Health and Education Acts are examples of Statute Law.

Other forms of law are incorporated in the Church (Ecclesiastical Law), the Army (Martial Law) and the legal and medical professions which normally, however, hand over to the civil authority major offenders against the Criminal Law.

This book will deal mainly with the sphere of Criminal Law as the growth of Law and Order in England is traced from Anglo-Saxon times to the present day. Civil Law and other forms of law will only be briefly mentioned. The emphasis will lie on law and law enforcement, as well as the causes which gave rise to disorder. Some of the points raised during this survey of how English society has dealt with disorder and the criminal element, are still burning issues today. In the final chapter discussion of a few of the controversial topics is attempted.

1 From Anglo-Saxon Times to the End of the Middle Ages

When the Romans withdrew their legions from Northern Europe to help defend Rome from barbarian onslaughts, Britain suffered as much as any country from the break-down of established order and civilisation. The repeated invasions of Northern invaders, such as the Norsemen, the Angles and the Saxons caused widespread chaos. Indeed, in the so-called 'Dark Ages' it seemed that only within the sheltered walls of monasteries could one find peace and security and what little learning there was; and even these places were subject to plundering and burning. Despite this, various societies of men existed, albeit under constant fear of disruption, and the different Kingdoms into which England was divided, such as Wessex, Kent and Mercia, formulated their own rules and laws to help maintain stability.

Anglo-Saxon law is very complex, partly because it came from so many different sources, and Alfred the Great, in his attempt to form a comprehensive code, employed a mixture of laws drawn from various clans, peoples and kingdoms. The law of that time is difficult and obscure, and we find it hard to imagine how our forefathers viewed it. In our relatively settled society of today we tend to take the

1 The King's Court or Witan. This early eleventh-century picture was meant to illustrate the story of Joseph. (In the Middle Ages most illustrations were done by monks and people attached to the Church.) It shows the attempt by an Anglo-Saxon to depict Pharaoh's court. Because the artist had little idea what ancient Egyptians looked like, he portrayed an Anglo-Saxon king and his court—except that he gave them pointed caps, which was, in fact, the dress of medieval Jews. The sword is usually symbolic of power, especially of jurisdiction.

law for granted. We naturally think in terms of a community which is peaceable and obedient for most of the time, regulated and supervised by a body of police. We also assume that the law governs many of an individual's actions and is usually already established, and that one can find it out and often read it up. To help one, if necessary, there is a large body of people: policemen to call upon in an emergency, lawyers and solicitors to defend one's interests; judges to sum up, and a jury to hear and give a verdict on one's case. In fact we live in a society where there is a professional class dedicated to administering the law.

None of these attributes of the law existed before the Norman Conquest in the form we have come to know them. There was no general habit of obedience, no settled code of laws, nor people whose sole job it was to enforce them. In a society which prized personal valour and military prowess above most other qualities, crime and violence were regarded as everyday occurrences. (The aim of every Norseman was to die whilst fighting bravely for his lord: he was then assured a place in Valhalla—the home of the gods and brave spirits.)

By the tenth century England was divided much as it is today, into shires. Each shire contained smaller districts called 'hundreds' in the South and Midlands and elsewhere called 'wapentakes'. These in turn were subdivided into 'townships' or 'vills' about the size of a modern parish. Communities were usually isolated, and in an agrarian society there was little commerce or industry; the law, and the way it was administered, was primitive. A 'court' would usually be held in each 'hundred' once a month and a 'shire court' two or three times a year. These courts were rather like public assemblies and every free man was obliged to attend his local court.

Kinship Before the tenth century if an injury was done to anyone, it was up to the injured party or his relatives or 'kindred' to avenge the wrong. If a man were killed, it was the kindred's duty to take vengeance on the slayer or his kindred, or to extract compensation. Fear of the action of a man's kindred was of great importance in maintaining order, and up to the Norman Conquest Anglo-Saxon law regarded homicide as the affair of the kindred. They were entitled to receive the *wergild* (or 'man price') for any of their members slain. This idea of the legal worth of a person was even expressed in terms of numbers of cattle. Social classes were sometimes spoken of as men worth so much money—e.g. 6, 12 or 100 shillings.

There were many offences for which no compensation (or *bot*) could be given. In the tenth century, as the importance of the kindred was undermined by the growth of tithings and lordship, the number of crimes considered 'botless' increased. These were always punishable by death or mutilation and the criminal's property was forfeited to the King. Thus by the early eleventh century one finds King Canute listing as 'botless' crimes (breaches of the King's Peace) such offences as ambush, housebreaking and failing to join the army when called upon. Gradually the King's Peace was extended in scope—especially during the Norman period—until it was claimed that any major crime was an offence against the King even if he was in no way affected by it.

2 The administration of justice, as depicted by the East Anglian monk Matthew Paris in the thirteenth century. It shows Alexander the Great having the murderers of Darius hung. Notice the bent right knee, the pose drawn by artists to depict the King or person administering justice.

Mutual Responsibility

To keep lawlessness and violence to a minimum the Anglo-Saxon kings and Danish overlords had employed what we might call a system of mutual responsibility. Much of the responsibility for local law and order rested with the thanes or local chieftains. They were required by the King to bring robbers before the courts or make good the victim's loss, and so it was in their own interest to either maintain good order, or find the criminal. Often the landless free men who were not attached to a thane were obliged to form associations of ten homesteads called 'tithings' and they elected from amongst themselves a chief called a 'headborough' or 'borsholder' (later 'alderman') who was responsible for the rest. Alfred the Great expanded this principle so that all members of such groups were held responsible for any members who broke the law and all shared in paying the fines which might be imposed. Thus each had an incentive to see that the rest kept to the laws. At first this system was labelled 'Peace of the Folk', but later—especially after the Norman Conquest—the responsibility for keeping law and order throughout the Kingdom was acknowledged as that of the ruler, or King, and was known as the 'King's Peace' (see above).

The Influence of the Normans

At first William the Conqueror and his successors tried to maintain the existing system of mutual and local responsibility for keeping the peace; there was no desire to change anything which ensured order in the newly acquired kingdom.

William I and Henry I insisted that the courts of shire or 'hundred' should be held regularly as they had been in the past. William the Conqueror broke new ground when he founded the church's own ecclesiastical courts (which in some respects have lasted to the present day). However, the expansion of the power of the monarch in Norman times caused considerable change in the way the country was governed. Whereas the Anglo-Saxon kings, despite great efforts by Edward the Confessor and Harold, had exercised little control over the law, William I, Henry I and Henry II extended their hold over the country and with it their role in both formulating and maintaining the laws. In Anglo-Saxon times the King had occasionally been advised by a small group of important men called the 'Witan'. The Normans created a group of semi-professional, skilled administrators known as the *Curia Regis* which gradually became a law court and increased in authority as the

9

King's power grew stronger. The King's coronation oath involved an undertaking to be responsible for the maintenance of peace and this meant ensuring justice and gave the monarch the opportunity to extend the sphere of this justice. Domesday Book is an example of the achievement of the *Curia Regis*. It illustrates the determination of the King to know what were the resources of his acquired kingdom and how much it was possible to exact in the form of land-tax. The revenue was to be collected by the sheriffs (or shire-reeves), the King's representatives in the county, and paid, together with other taxes and fines, into a central treasury of the King's household. This central treasury gradually became a separate department of the *Curia Regis*, called the 'Barons of the Exchequer' and later still divided into separate courts, such as the Exchequer court. This centralising tendency of the Normans meant that beside the expansion of civil (exchequer) justice, the machinery for dealing with criminal offences also expanded.

Despite widespread antipathy to the royal officials, the Normans, as they extended their authority over the country, exercised even firmer control. Under Henry II and Edward I (called 'the Lawmaker'), the laws became more systematised, and by the end of the thirteenth century all major cases had been taken away from the ancient local courts of the manor, 'hundred' and shire. They were, by then, tried by the King's justices who travelled round the country on a regular circuit—as they still do today. At the local level, the lord of the manor still presided over the court-leet; but this dealt only with such petty matters as local taxation disputes, scandal-mongering or the shifting of boundary posts.

Henry II's Achievements 1154–89

Henry II's reign is notable for firm, even strong government, and the real attempts he made to combat the lawlessness of his time. He loved legal argument and often sat in person to give judgement in his own court. Frequent crimes and the seizure of property by force were commonplace and in large measure these were due to the anarchy of Stephen's reign. Under Henry II the 'King's Peace' began to be thought of as a form of protection for all. It became a right of trial which could easily be obtained by simply alleging a breach of the King's Peace. The King's courts began to acquire a reputation for speedy efficiency and justice which had the advantage also of being cheaper than thitherto. This forced the dispute or case to go before a royal court, usually that of the justices 'in eyre' who presided periodically at the shire courts, in the King's name. Henry II also did more than anyone to initiate the policy of replacing trial by ordeal and battle with trial by a jury of twelve men. The number of wrongs considered crimes increased rapidly and by the reign of King John, little, except misconduct of a petty kind, was left to the local and private courts.

The edict entitled *Assize of Clarendon* and issued by Henry II in 1166 illustrates his determination to tackle the lawlessness of the time. He ordered twelve men from every 'hundred', and four from every village to come before his sheriffs and his justices to state on oath whom they believed to be murderers, robbers, thieves and the people who afforded them shelter. Those under suspicion were to be tried before the justices only; to submit themselves to compurgation, or the ordeal by water, and even though they might be proved 'not guilty', they were to leave the

3 Taking the oath, in the fourteenth century. Even though it withdrew its support from trial by ordeal in 1215, the Church has played an important role in the administration of the law ever since. Even today witnesses are required to swear to tell the truth upon the Bible. People in the Middle Ages were much more religious than today and to swear an oath was extremely serious. One result was that in the early Middle Ages, if one could collect enough people of good standing who were prepared to vouch for one upon oath ('compurgators'), then often the case would be considered finished.

country within eight days for being of ill repute with their neighbours.

The Assize of Northampton (1178) added arson and forgery to the list of offences and increased the mutilations inflicted on the convicted.

Traditionally Magna Carta has been regarded as a list of Englishmen's liberties extorted from and sealed by King John. It is a remarkable document, if only because it illustrates how far the role of law had been developed in society. In condemning the arbitrary actions of John, the barons stated firmly that there was established law binding on all people and that this should be followed by all. Before long Henry Bracton in 1250 was claiming that 'the King should be under God and the Law'. For him to state that the King was below the law illustrates the importance attached to the idea of an universal power or 'natural law' by which men must be guided in their conduct, both the mighty and the meek. *Magna Carta, 1215*

Two extracts from Magna Carta are of interest. King John promised that:

> No merchant shall be filched of his merchandise, and no villein deprived of his agricultural implements; and that no man should be appointed a justiciary, constable, sheriff or bailiff unless he understood the law of the land and was prepared to observe it.

A clause outlining the legal powers of authority in any form was granted also:

> No free man may be arrested or imprisoned or desseised or outlawed or exiled, or in any way brought to ruin, save by the legal judgement of his peers or by the law of the land.

Another landmark in medieval criminal law is Edward I's Statute of Winchester.

This statute illustrates the concern with which the government viewed crime and disorder throughout the kingdom. Much of the trouble, by the thirteenth century, stemmed from the lawlessness in the towns. Since 1066 the population had almost *Edward I's Statute of Winchester, 1285* doubled, from roughly 1,500,000 to 3,000,000 and the towns absorbed much of the increase, causing strain to the existing methods of law enforcement. This statute had two important provisions.

Firstly, every borough was required to keep *Watch and Ward*, which included the closing and watching of the town or city gates from sunset to sunrise and all hosts were to be responsible for the conduct of their guests. The responsibility for keeping the peace was thus again placed on all males.

Hue and Cry also became a statutory obligation. If any man who had committed a wrong tried to evade justice, a hue and cry was to be raised after him and all men were bound to leave what they were doing and give chase. Anyone not doing so was liable to be tried along with the offender.

New officers called 'Conservators of the Peace' were appointed to enforce these laws, and to assist them two High Constables were appointed for each 'hundred' and franchise with specific orders like: 'All suspicious night-walkers are to be arrested and detained by the watch.'

Justices of the Peace and Constables

Edward III in 1332 empowered parish constables to arrest people suspected of slaughter, felonies and robberies, and to take them to the sheriff. The office of constable had been known in the thirteenth century, connected with the militia but from the time of Edward III petty constables, whose office was purely civil, really became the assistants to the justices of the peace.

The office of J.P. can be traced back to Henry II's 'custodes pacis' and more exactly to 1195 when Richard I appointed by proclamation certain knights 'to swear to the King' all men over fifteen to keep the peace, but in 1360 a statute specifically 'assigned for the keeping of the peace in every county one lord and with him three or four of the most worthy in the county, with some learned in the law'. It also authorised them not only to arrest and imprison offenders but 'to hear and determine at the King's suit all manner of felonies and trespasses done in the same county'.

By 1363 they were ordered to meet in session every three months. This was the origin of the present 'quarter sessions' and it relieved the royal judges of much onerous work. At first the office of J.P. had been meant only to deal with local disturbances and the apprehension of criminals, but gradually, as the monarchy realised their worth, extra administrative duties and judicial powers were added. By the Tudor period it was a post carrying a heavy burden of responsibility. The parish constables were unpaid except for certain fees, and the office was compulsory on every capable parishioner apart from exempted people like clergy, knights, clerks and women. As the duties increased, so the post became more unpopular and people paid deputies to take their place, if they could possibly afford it.

Methods of Trial

A man accused of a crime might bring witnesses to the court to prove his innocence; in Saxon times 'oath-helpers' or 'compurgators', if worthy citizens, might clear the defendant. If there was doubt about the rights of the case the accused might undergo the *Trial by Ordeal*, when the judgement of God was invoked to pronounce guilt or innocence.

In the ordeal of cold water, the accused was given holy water to drink and then he was lowered into water. If he floated, he was considered guilty! Other forms of ordeal were often carried out in the church, with the two opposing groups of the lawsuit present to ensure that no trickery was attempted. In the ordeal by fire, the accused carried a glowing bar of iron for nine feet; in the ordeal by hot water he plunged his hand into boiling water to take out a stone. His hand was then bandaged and sealed. If, after three days, the wound had healed without festering, the man was cleared of the charge. Another method of trial and introduced by the Normans was that of combat, where the accused and accuser fought each other till one submitted or the accused proved his innocence by holding out until sunset. Many people hired champions to fight for them! Trial by battle was finally abolished in 1820.

Trials by ordeal died out during the thirteenth century except for certain types of dispute, especially as from the reign of Henry II there grew up the system of *Trial by Jury*. (Juries began as information-giving groups but in time they were required to decide whether, on the evidence of the prosecution, the case was worthy of a trial.) In 1215 the Pope forbade all clergy to take part in the proceeding of trial by ordeal. Trial by battle could not be used when the King himself was the prosecutor, and the practice of compurgation was too open to lies and bribery. However, trial by jury was not as immediately popular as might be thought. The accused was asked to consent to a jury of his neighbours, for it was believed that in some ways, he stood a better chance of acquittal under the old ordeal which might reveal God on his side, even though his neighbours condemned him. Notorious evil-doers who refused to go before a jury were usually compelled to do so by the use of torture. This use of torture was called 'peine et forte dure' and was authorised by a statute of Edward I in 1275. This law was not finally abolished

4   *Trial by Ordeal—the combat.* Although sanctified by the Church and hedged about with civil and legal ceremonies, the trial by combat was hardly the best way of ensuring justice. God was considered to be on the side of the guiltless man but this came to mean less and less when champions could be hired to fight one's legal battles.

5 Men in prison and stocks: a twelfth-century copy of an earlier drawing done at Christchurch, Canterbury. The most usual gaols were the dungeons of castles, where lords might incarcerate prisoners, but imprisonment as such was not very common in the Middle Ages. Prisoners were bound with rope as iron was much too expensive: nails were a highly prized commodity and might be found mentioned in a will!

until 1870, although from 1772 onwards, if a person 'stood mute', he was judged guilty and punished!

From the time of William the Conqueror the church in England had maintained its own courts for all clerks in Holy Orders, and this could mean most semi-literate men, for the church had a virtual monopoly of learning. A clerk accused of most crimes except treason might claim *Benefit of Clergy* and he could be tried only by the courts of the church, which were usually more lenient in their punishments. A reading test would be given to a man claiming Benefit of Clergy—verse 1 of the 51st Psalm. It became known as the 'neck verse' because the ability to read it saved many a man from the gallows. For example, in 1328, of four men accused of theft one claimed benefit of clergy and he was the only one who was not hanged!

One refuge for the medieval criminal was the taking of *Sanctuary*. A church or sacred building was considered a place safe from arrest. After forty days, however, he could be blockaded and starved unless he chose to 'abjure the realm', i.e. swear to leave the country for ever, from the nearest port and by the first vessel.

Medieval Punishments

Edward I is renowned as a lawmaker, yet when out hunting in the King's forest he ordered the ears of a peasant to be cut off; the man's offence was that he was trespassing on royal hunting grounds, and savage penalties were usually inflicted on anyone found damaging the game or in any way violating their breeding grounds. The King's companions would have thought nothing amiss with this infliction of punishment. Today we might think the punishments then meted out to criminals crude and inhuman, but some of the ideas involved are still being mooted in present-day debates over punishments and the question of reparation to victims or the victims' relatives.

In Saxon times a man who killed another was liable to a triple penalty whether he had killed by accident, self-defence or murder. He might have to

1. Pay money to the victim's next-of-kin by way of compensation.
2. Pay an equal sum to the thane for the loss of a servant killed.
3. Pay an equal sum to the King for the violence done to the King's Peace.

But some crimes such as arson, house-breaking, open theft and treachery to one's lord were called 'botless' crimes, for which no compensation could be offered. Murder was punishable by death and usually the convicted man was hanged, drawn and quartered. Thefts of anything above the value of one shilling were also capital offences. (A man's wergild or 'man price' might be valued at only just above this!)

For offences like cheating in business, selling loaves under-weight and bad workmanship, people were punished in the stocks or the pillory. Even the scandal-mongers or the malicious gossips got their deserts by being ducked in the local pond. Sometimes there was imprisonment or mutilation, as when, according to the *Chronicle of London*, three men who took two prisoners from the custody of the 'serjeant of London' had their right hands cut off. Often the punishment was made to fit the crime; a vintner who sold bad wine might be required to drink it and have the rest poured over him.

6 *A baker being drawn to the pillory,* bound hand and foot to a rudimentary sledge. He wears round his neck the underweight loaf for which he is being punished. The regulation weight was fixed by 'Assizes'—a form of price and quality guarantee. The same regulations governed the sale of cloth—hence 'regulation width'. Millers too were notorious rascals, as Chaucer tells us in the Prologue to *The Canterbury Tales*. (Notice the early form of harness and the obvious crudeness of the sledge.)

The worst of punishments was reserved for men convicted of high treason, or the crime of conspiring against the King. Treason was not a statutory offence before the fourteenth century. It was introduced at the insistence of the barons, for their own protection. In Edward III's time the guilty man was drawn to the place of execution on the ground, hanged by the neck and then cut down alive; the entrails were taken out and burned while he was yet alive. The head was cut off and the body divided into four parts, which were at the King's disposal. Women were sometimes strangled and in later centuries burned, as were convicted witches. In France, Joan of Arc was burned at the stake for being an heretic and a witch. Usually, as a warning to others, the mutilated bodies of criminals were fixed to the castle walls or exhibited at a gate or bridge leading to the town. The punishment ordered could be varied in severity to suit the case. Breaking on the wheel or burning at the stake could be made a quick or slow death, according to the way the executioner wanted to please the audience.

The End of the Middle Ages

By the fourteenth century the strong government and impetus to centralisation exhibited by William I, Henry I, Henry II and Edward I had begun to degenerate. When the King was weak, the institutions controlling law and order in the community were taken over by over-powerful individuals with armed men in their pay. The decline of justice and good order are reflected in the acknowledged evils of the time. Lords enlisted private armies or fighting servants who wore the uniform and emblem of their master. This system was known as 'livery'. When his followers finished up in the law courts—which still functioned—the lord would bring pressure to bear on juries, often by force and intimidation or bribery. This process of obtaining justice was called 'embracery'. These abuses undermined the whole system of law-enforcement which had grown up through the Middle Ages. As men resorted to violence, so others were compelled to take up arms to meet it. Often, in the absence of strong royal authority and the certainty of punishment, a lord would break up a law session by violence. For example, in 1439 the justices of a special commission could not hold their session in the Bedford Town Hall because Lord Fanhope interrupted proceedings with sixty armed followers and caused an uproar. Even the monarch was capable of obstructing the course of justice: in 1451, when Lord Moleyns was indicted for an armed attack upon the Paston's Manor of Gresham, the sheriff of Norfolk received 'writing from the Kyng that he shall make such a panell to aquyte the Lord Moleyns'—and acquitted he was!

The breakdown of local government could only be remedied by an increase in royal authority. Edward IV tried hard to bring peace and order to his kingdom. In 1462 he appeared in person in the Court of King's Bench and he accompanied his judges round the shires for several years but the lull in the civil war was too brief for proper order to be restored. Only when the battle for the throne between the Houses of York and Lancaster had been resolved, could there be a real chance for a powerful king to get his country in order and the start was made when Henry VII ascended the throne in 1485.

At the end of the Middle Ages it seemed that the efforts of law-makers like Edward I had been in vain. Though the institutions of law and order had not disappeared they were being abused and the justice of the day perverted. No doubt, throughout the period stretching from Saxon times to the Tudors, law enforcement was a very rough and ready process by our standards. But much was achieved. The Tudors were able to build upon the foundations laid by the strong medieval kings. As the state became more powerful in the sixteenth century, so did the organs of government and nowhere is this more obvious than in the office

8 *A market-place execution,* from Froissart's *Chronicles* (late fourteenth-century). Afterwards the body was cut in four pieces and then nailed to the gates of the city. Notice: (1) The condemned man has the opportunity to confess to either the Dominican Friar (in black), or the Franciscan Friar (in brown); (2) The open-air pulpit on the right; (3) The high pillory in the centre. One can see from this how popular a public execution was—people are in their 'Sunday best' clothes. One might invite special guests if one's house overlooked the place of execution.

of J.P. The Tudors were to take over and modify the existing means of government and legal machinery and adapt them to their problems which faced them, just as the Normans had assimilated the Anglo-Saxon system.

One obvious legacy of the Middle Ages is the Watch and Ward system set up by the Statute of Winchester in 1285. This was to last almost unchanged for six hundred years—it survived in London even after the formation of Peel's police in 1829. Of much more importance, however, is the body of common law which was passed on. Out of the *Curia Regis* of the twelfth century there had grown up two main courts of law which, by the fourteenth century, were separated from the King's household. The court of King's Bench—officially 'curia regis coram rege' (king's court held in his presence)—dealt with criminal matters and all cases affecting the King's interests. The King still made his presence felt and might, like Edward IV, sit in person, but the close connection was gradually lost. The court of Common Pleas, by the fourteenth century, was a completely separate institution held regularly at Westminster. Judges became specialists dealing with civil disputes between party and party, particularly when it came to disputes concerning land. In addition there was the Court of Exchequer to deal with revenue cases and the Court of Chancery which handled civil matters such as property, contracts, wills and the like.

Further Reading   D. Whitelock, *The Beginning of English Society* (Pelican History of England 1952)
D. M. Stenton, *English Society in the Early Middle Ages* (Pelican History of England 1951)

2 The Tudor and Stuart Periods 1485–1688

The accession to the throne of Henry VII in 1485 saw the first real attempts at checking the disorder which had prevailed throughout much of the fifteenth century. In his firm and decisive way Henry, largely to secure his own throne, steadily enforced the law and suppressed those who had threatened the peace of the country. He recovered the powers belonging to feudal kings and, by the imposition of heavy fines, he put an end to the menace of over-mighty subjects. In this battle for the restoration of order the King found that the existing laws against violence were usually sufficient for him to keep the unruly lord or knight in check; his main task was to ensure that the courts were powerful enough to apply the laws sternly and impartially. That so little legislation was needed, illustrates the fact that the real fault had lain in the weakness at the top of society—in the Crown.

Of the acts he passed, one in 1485 prohibited hunting in disguise since it was supposed in the past to have given occasion for riots and murders. The procedure employed in catching and punishing murderers was tightened up in 1487; the abduction of women (heiresses usually!) without their consent was forbidden. In 1495 four separate acts tried to solve one of the greatest problems of all—corruption and the returning of false verdicts by the courts. The Tudors were continually troubled by this. One of the difficulties involved was the power of the sheriff who empanelled juries and kept prisoners in custody. Often he would be influenced by the local magnates and this tended to make him useless to the central government. Laws were passed in 1495 and 1504 recalling sheriffs to their duties, but the importance of this office declined throughout the sixteenth century as the justice of the peace, much more amenable to central control, took over extra responsibility for local government.

Little of what Henry VII did in his battle to restore order was new. Most of the laws had been in existence before and all that was needed was a policy of rigorous enforcement. This he supplied. The success of his struggle with the most obvious source of disorder—the power of the over-mighty subjects—was only part of the task. These, in any case, had always been few in number, and the Wars of the Roses had considerably thinned their ranks.

The greatest problem was to get men to settle their disputes in a court of law rather than by force of arms. The Tudor age was very much one of quick tempers and violence and the government of the day was continually troubled by the mass of small affrays and quarrels, the stabbings and cudgellings and localised riots. Not until the nineteenth century and the creation of an efficient and powerful police force was there much chance of preventing trouble; all that could be done, it was thought, was to make the consequences of crimes and violence extremely unpleasant. Savage penalties were inflicted in the hope that fear of punishment would deter criminals and prevent actions leading to disorder.

Local Government and Justices of the Peace

In the sphere of local government Henry VII and his successors had to rely almost exclusively on the part-time services of amateur administrators. Just as it was every man's duty to take up arms for his country's defence, so every competent male citizen was expected to play a part in local government. Within each unit of local government—manor, parish, township, hundred or shire—there were offices to fill, taxes to collect, juries to be manned. Thus the strong rule of the Tudors rested at base on a broad measure of self-government. In the office of the J.P. which can be traced back as far as the twelfth century (see Chapter 1), the Tudors found the ideal instrument for their purposes. The commission had to be renewed frequently, so there was little risk in founding a power independent of the central government: it cost practically nothing to operate, and it was staffed by local worthies often of aristocratic connection who could command obedience more by respect than force.

In addition to the J.P.'s primary task of preserving local law and order, parliament after parliament added fresh duties which made the J.P. supreme over every other local official or institution, from the sheriff to the constable. The rising prestige and expanding scope of the office were reflected in the growing number of treatises dealing with the office, such as *The Boke of Justyces of Peas* published in 1506. So busy did the J.P. become under the Tudors that by 1581 William Lombard wrote complaining that the weight and bewildering complexity of duties was hindering the J.P.'s efficiency. 'How many Justices', he asked, 'may now suffice (without breaking their backs) to bear so many, not Loads but Stacks of Statutes, that have been laid upon them?'

The J.P.s in the fifteenth century had often neglected their office, and the Tudors set about making this important link in the chain of government stronger. More care was taken over appointments and Henry VII helped to make the office of J.P. the recognised first step (apprenticeship it could be called) in a gentleman's public career.

Thus, Tudor government under Henry VII basically consisted of twenty or thirty important men sitting at the centre of affairs in Council or Star Chamber, with six to seven hundred J.P.s covering the country in petty and quarter sessions. These men, in early Tudor times, were the chief agents of royal power at their respective levels.

The Duties of the Justices

Besides their important functions in the administration of justice, the control of vagabonds and beggars, the working of the poor law, the licensing of ale-houses and the regulation of labour and wages, the justices were charged by Statute with various duties concerned with policing their area. These tasks covered a wide range from trespass and the stealing of partridges and the eggs of hawks and swans, to imprisoning people who wrote, sang, or spoke 'any phantastical or false prophecy' with the purpose of making rebellions. They not only dealt with trivial offences like the robbing of orchards but were called upon to enforce the religious laws of the day.

There was no doubt that the justices were hard worked, both in the towns, which were expanding rapidly in the sixteenth century, and in the country, where they had to deal with the serious problem of vagrancy. One contemporary writer states

20

9 The burning of Anne Askewe and Jacels, Smithfield Market, London in 1546. An outstanding example of the sporadic persecution persisting in the last years of Henry VIII's reign was the torture, trial and burning of Anne Askewe. She went to the stake for her denial of the Church doctrine of 'transubstantiation'.

that 'Henry VIII caused to be hanged of great thieves and petty thieves three score and twelve thousand'. Though an exaggeration, the comment reveals that vast numbers were troubling the peace in society. If the courts were busy, some of the magistrates paid themselves handsomely for their hard work. An Elizabethan writer complained that some men became magistrates with the express purpose of lining their 'pokets'. He describes the justice of the peace as 'a living creature that for half a dozen chickens would dispense a whole dozen of penal Statutes'. No doubt the office lent itself to a large measure of corruption and bribery, especially as no real stipend was attached to the post. Often, too, their assistants would be poor substitute constables like Elbow in Shakespeare's *Measure for Measure*. Dogberry and Verges and the sleep-loving watchman in *Much Ado About Nothing* are also fairly typical of the early seventeenth century. 'We will rather sleep than talk—we know what belongs to a watch.' But with little means at their disposal to maintain law and order—beyond the deterrent of savage punishments—the justices of the peace had their work cut out. Contemporary documents illustrate vividly the kind of criminal operations prevalent in London in 1585. In many ways the following extract from a letter by Fleetwood to Lord Burghley foreshadows Dickens' *Oliver Twist* and *Fagin* by over two hundred years:

10 *The Elizabethan Underworld.* On the left is a chief of beggars in the guise of respectability and on the right he assumes the tattered garments of a poor beggar. These beggars, often the able-bodied men who could not find honest work, were a serious menace to law-abiding citizens and the local authorities. The course taken by the magistrate, that of whipping the vagrant and sending him towards the parish of his birth, did little to remedy the situation.

that one Wotton, a gentilman borne, and sometyme a marchauntt man of good credyte, who fallings by tyme into decaye kept an Alehouse . . . and procured all the Cuttpurses abowt the Cittie to repaire to his said howse. There was a schole howse set upp to learne younge boyes to cutt purses. There were hung up two devises, the one was a pockett, the other was a purse. The pockett had in yt certain cownters and was hunge abowte with hawkes bells, and over the toppe did hannge a little sacring bell; and he that could take owt a cownter without any noyse, was allowed to be a publique Foyster; and he that could take a peece of sylver owt of the purse without the noyse of any of the bells, he was ad-judged a judiciall Nypper. Nota that a Foyster is a Pick-pockett, and a Nypper is termed a Pickepurse, or a Cutpurse.

A few of the phrases used by the Elizabethan underworld are interesting:

A 'cursitor' was the name given to a vagabond; a 'ruffler' was a sturdy beggar; an 'upright man' was the chief of a begging community—a Fagin-type role; a 'prigger of prances' was a horse-thief; an 'Abraham man'—one who feigned madness; a 'dummerer'—one who feigned dumbness; a 'coney-catcher' meant a confidence trickster.

Punishments Londoners were accustomed to seeing traitors hung, drawn and quartered, heretics burned at the stake and thieves hung. In fact these were one of the main attractions for the enjoyment of a visitor to the capital city. Most of the punishments inflicted had been employed in the Middle Ages but certain offences, like that of treason and nonconformity in the religion of the monarch, carried penalties which re-flected the growth of the state and the authoritarian rule of the Tudors. The treason law was stretched by Henry VIII to include that of poisoning anyone and

22

the penalty was death by boiling! It was recorded that a 'man was soddyne in a cautherne (i.e. boiled in a cauldron) in Smithfield and let up and down divers times till he was dead, because he would have poisoned divers persons'. Speaking seditious words also meant death or the loss of both ears. Many people went to the stake to be burned, rather than give up the practice of their religious beliefs— especially in the reign of the Catholic Queen Mary.

But dangerous though it was to refuse to obey the supreme authority of the land—the monarch, reigning through Parliament—the spectacular deaths of prisoners and martyrs only served to hide the real problem that the Tudors faced. This was the problem of the poor; it was more insoluble because the authorities had few ideas as to its causes and even fewer about how to remedy the havoc which hordes of vagabonds and 'sturdy' beggars brought in their wake as they tramped the country looking for work and bread.

The Poor and Vagrancy

Throughout the sixteenth century society was changing rapidly. The country was getting richer and the population, almost static after the Black Death of 1348 and throughout most of the fifteenth century, was growing again at a fast rate. Though the rich lived lavishly (we can see evidence of this from the Tudor houses still standing) the poor were often worse off than before. Unemployment, especially in the middle decades of the century and the nineties, was widespread and presented grave problems to the authorities. The rise in prices, the dissolution of the monasteries, the enclosure of land for the profitable rearing of sheep for the cloth trade— these and other factors, when taken with the growth of population, caused widespread beggary. Most authorities tackled the problem vigorously; their answer was to whip persistent vagrants or burn them through the ear and send them packing back to the parish of their birth. Private charity by churches and noblemen, the traditional helpers of the destitute, was no longer able to cope with the pressing need for poor relief. Towns like London and Norwich led the way by imposing a compulsory poor rate. With the money hospitals, houses of correction and asylums

11 *Vagabond being whipped and beaten,* to encourage him to lead an honest life. No easy quest when the population was increasing rapidly and there was lack of work. Robert Crawley in 1550 tells how two beggars might talk to one another:

No man would pity me but for my sore leg,
Wherefore if I were whole I might in vain beg.
I might be constrained to labour and sweat
And perhaps sometimes with scourges be beat.

Already a distinction was drawn between the weak and aged, and the 'sturdy' beggar who was workshy.

12 *The stocks in Tudor England.* A commonplace sight in towns and villages —a punishment of public disgrace reserved for minor offences such as telling tales, vagabondage, etc.

were established. Eventually, due mainly to the scarcity and distress caused by a series of bad harvests from 1594–97, Parliament passed a bill—the celebrated Elizabethan Poor Law—establishing a compulsory poor rate throughout the country. It gave justices of the peace the power to appoint overseers of the poor in every parish, to set the able-bodied to work, to provide for the infirm poor and to bind poor children as apprentices to a trade.

That the state, in the form of an act of Parliament, should concern itself so much with the poor, illustrates how much the authorities feared the disorder and violence which the wandering beggars caused. Contemporary documents are full of reference to the problem. A writer in Henry VII's time complained 'that in no country in Christendom, for the number of people, you shall find so many beggars as be here in England, and now more than have been before this time which argueth plain great poverty'. Richard Hitchcock in 1580 spoke of 'the great and huge numbers of beggars and vagabonds' and of soldiers who had fought in the wars with 'invincible minds' but cannot get work and either go abroad, 'or else they tarry in England, hanging is the end of the most part of them'.

Savage punishments were directed against rogues and vagabonds especially during the reign of Edward VI. An act of 1547 provided that on conviction before two justices of the peace, they might be branded 'in the breast' and reduced to slavery for the space of two years; on a conviction of escape there was a second branding, 'on the forehead or the ball of the cheek', and the slavery became perpetual. If a second escape occurred, this entailed death as a felon. Harrison, in *A Description of England* in 1577 tells of the fate of the vagabond:

> The roge being apprehended, committed to prison, and tried in the next assises . . . if he happen to be convicted for a vagabond, either by inquest of office, or the testimonie of two honest and credible witnesses upon their oths, he is then immediately adjudged to be greevouslie whipped and burned through the gristle of the right eare, with an hot iron of the compasse of an inch about, as a manifestation of his wicked life and due punishment received for the same.

Many of the wandering poor who were able to work were provided for in the Houses of Correction—later called workhouses—but the problem of destitute and lawless bands roaming the country caused concern for another two hundred years.

13 Court of Wards and Liveries sitting in the reign of Elizabeth. This is one of the many courts or departments set up by the Tudors in an effort to organise the state. This court administered the feudal income of the Crown. By Elizabethan times the monarch still retained the right to be paid a fine known as 'relief' when an heir took over his lands. If the heir was under age, he and his lands were subject to wardship (these were controlled by the King who enjoyed the revenue until he came of age) and to livery (the fine paid to recover the lands out of wardship). Wardships could be sold for cash. The Tudors made good use of this ancient right for they were usually short of money, especially as the value of the Crown's revenue declined.

Today heiresses under 21 can still be made wards of court usually to prevent them being married, until they attain the legal age of responsibility.

Each community had its quota of work-shy people and there was no doubt that many preferred to live by their wits or obtain relief from the authorities rather than settle down. Imprisonment, though, was to be avoided at all costs, for a man might be left in prison for years without a trial, and once there, a contemporary said, men 'were lodged like hogs and fed like dogs'. Another spoke of the 'syckness of the prisons' which came of the corruption of the air, 'as many men be together in a little room, having but little open air'.

25

14 *The martyrdom of Catholic priests,* from John Foxe's 'Book of Martyrs,' *Actes and Monuments.* 'Bloody Queen Mary' had caused nearly 300 Protestants to be burned for their faith. This created an undying hatred for the Pope and Roman Catholicism which lasted for some 300 years. This illustration is from the later years of Queen Elizabeth. The persecution of Catholics was vigorous throughout her reign. With the threat of foreign invasion from Catholic Spain, the Catholic 'mass priests' who entered the country were put to the stake on a charge of treason. Elizabeth herself claimed that no one was persecuted in England because of his religion, but because they obeyed a Papal Bull of 1570 issued by Pius V which declared Elizabeth excommunicated and deposed. About 250 died for the Catholic faith; the ones illustrated above suffered the fate of those convicted of treason— that of being hung, drawn and quartered.

The harsh Poor Law did much to break up the bands of roving vagabonds who terrorised Elizabethan England. It did not prevent London becoming the magnet which attracted an underworld of casual labourers, beggars, criminals and unemployables. By restricting the movement of labour in the rural areas because of the fear of vagrancy, the authorities were preventing the real solution to the problem of the poor, that of absorbing them into expanding industry. Under James I and Charles I there was a permanent background of social unrest and in a time of crisis, such as a famine, large-scale unemployment or a break-down of government, disorder could so easily occur. In 1622 groups of unemployed in Gloucestershire raided the houses of the rich, demanding money and seizing food. With no organised police force and no standing army, normal law and order was maintained by letting only the landed class bear arms. The gentry, said Sir Walter Raleigh 'are the garrisons of good order through the realm'. If one landed up before the magistrate there might be an empty basket displayed in front of him—for gifts in kind, from petitioners and offenders. This so-called 'basket' justice became well known in James I's reign.

Cromwellian Rule and the Legacy of Hatred of Strong Government

Matters were made worse, if anything, by the brief spell of military rule by Cromwell. Under his grandiose scheme for ruling England and keeping the peace the country was divided up into districts. In 1655, because of insurrectionary movements and assassination plots, he organised a local militia of 6,000 horsemen and placed them under the command of eleven 'Major-Generals' each controlling a district of from two to seven counties and having 500 men each. They were not really intended to supersede the local magistrates but to stimulate them into greater activity. However, their zeal for the reformation of public and private morals led to an irritating interference with personal freedom. As part of his policy of social reform, Cromwell produced in 1654 an Ordinance for the Reformation of Manners. This order suppressed cock-fighting since it was found 'to tend many times to the disturbance of the public peace' and to be 'commonly accompanied with gambling, drinking, swearing, quarrelling and other dissolute practices'. Another ordinance was aimed at 'challenges, duels and all provocations thereunto', for they, 'were a growing evil in this nation, displeasing to God, unbecoming Christians and contrary to all good order and government'. Other legislation provided for the 'better suppressing of drunkenness and profane swearing' among carmen, porters, watermen, and others 'at work upon the River of Thames, who are very ordinarily drunk and do . . . blaspheme'.

It is hardly surprising that so authoritarian a regime, under which spying was encouraged and the promotion of individual holiness attempted, should leave a legacy of distrust for central authority. Any plan to police the state efficiently immediately aroused in people memories of the military system adopted by Cromwell; it was thought preferable to have a certain amount of lawlessness in society rather than have individual freedoms taken away.

When the monarchy was restored in 1660 people looked forward to a time of less government and more freedom. This partly explains why the system of law enforcement changed so little up to the early nineteenth century. Charles II was responsible for some innovations, however. In 1663 by Act of Council a new force of paid night watchmen—popularly known as 'Charlies'—was instituted for

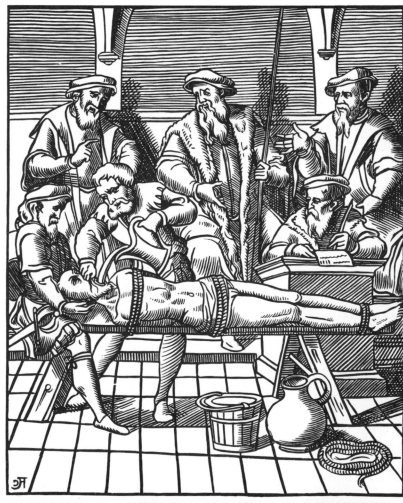

15 *The water torture:* a method of getting people to confess or stand trial that was more employed on the Continent than in England. A horrible torture as the victim's belly could distend until it burst.

the City of London. The King also arranged with a contractor for a lamp to be fitted at every tenth door in the more fashionable areas of London, mostly because at this time gangs of dissolute young men roamed the streets causing havoc to peaceful citizens. These groups largely made up of young noblemen were a form of irresponsible 'adventure' club and they gave themselves names like the Muns, Tityre Tus, Hestors, Nickers, Hawkubites and Mohocks. The 'Charlies' and the policing system generally was ridiculed as it proved more and more ineffective. The social position of the constable deteriorated further and it was just as well that the average constable was unaware of the powers entrusted to him by law.

The sixteenth and seventeeth centuries hold an important place in the history of English Law. Under the Tudors the role that Parliament played in the running of the country was enlarged. Various statutes and Acts of Parliament made legal Henry VIII's break with Rome and the establishment of the Church of England. By the end of the sixteenth century a good proportion of the M.P.s had received legal training at the Inns of Court and a trained opposition to royal measures grew up. The seventeenth century is notable for the struggle for supremacy between king and parliament, a struggle in which Charles I forfeited his head and crown, and James II his throne. Underlying this contest was the issue as to whether common law which had grown up over the centuries was more powerful than the law exercised by the King through his own Court of the Star Chamber and prerogative courts. By the end of the century common law had emerged triumphant and the judicial system was able to stand on its own feet. It was part of the constitutional settlement of 1688 that judges were to be independent of royal influence; they could not be dismissed as long as they did their work properly. Before this judges had held their posts at the King's pleasure and could be, and were, dismissed if judgements unfavourable to the Crown were pronounced.

16 *The watchman or bellman of London, 1616.* There were few enough watchmen, but they were the forerunners of the 'Charlies' introduced in 1663 by Charles II.

17 *The penitent murtherer'*. The illustration is self-explanatory. There was a tendency in the late seventeenth century to moralise naïvely about the evils of breaking the law. Much the same is one of the earliest English novels written at this time, Daniel Defoe's *Moll Flanders*, which gives a valuable insight into London's criminal underworld.

THE PENITENT MURTHERER

Another example of how common law triumphed over the power of the King is contained in the *Habeas Corpus Act* of 1679. This secured for the individual the right to be heard by a judge within twenty days at most from the time of arrest, and it incorporated the ancient right which could be traced back to Magna Carta. (This Act does not extend to Scotland but the subject there is protected by the Wrongus Imprisonment Act of 1701.) The Habeas Corpus Act is fundamental to the liberties of the individual and except during a government's emergency powers during the last World War, has only been suspended from 1794–1801 (see p. 45) in 1817 (see p. 54) and at the time of the Fenian Revolt in 1866.

A. V. Judges, *The Elizabethan Underworld* (Routledge 1930)   *Further Reading*

3 Eighteenth Century—'Out of Order'

It had been no easy task for the government to maintain law and order in the seventeenth century. The recurrent danger to society of the roving 'sturdy' beggars was somewhat solved but in its place had grown a potential source of disorder, that of a large section of the community living just about on the bread-line. This was the expanding class of unskilled industrial and agricultural labourers, which, in times of depression or bad harvest, was always a source of disorderly and anti-social behaviour. The devastations and upheavals caused by the Civil War made matters worse. It increased the growth of hatred for strict government. In the absence of central control, the freedom of the individual was enhanced; dangers arose when freedom became licence. The end of the seventeenth century sees the first mention of the problem of bands of riff-raff, urban poor and criminals causing disorder in the cities, especially in the capital. 'The reason . . . for which all government was at first appointed was to prevent mobs and rabbles in the world', said Daniel Defoe. The problem of the 'mob' was to grow worse in the eighteenth century.

At the start of George I's reign in 1715 the existing framework for ensuring local law and order was still basically medieval. The 'watch and ward' clause of the 1285 Statute of Winchester had enjoined all male citizens to serve their turn on the town watch without payment. But by 1715 many towns had no watchmen and, even when they did exist, their efficiency usually left much to be desired. In the country the justices tightened their grip and extended their influence, but in the towns the rapid rise of population caused great difficulties. Many town authorities, especially in the reign of George III, tried to improve their policing arrangements by getting local 'Improvement Acts' passed through Parliament. These authorised the appointment of 'Improvement Commissioners' responsible for the scavenging, lighting and paving of streets, as well as the police arrangements. In general, though, little positive action was taken to deal with the growing numbers of the criminal and lawless in society, especially in the urban areas.

Population Increase and Growing Urbanisation

Eighteenth-century England saw a period of greater change than even our parents have seen in their life-time. In 1700 there were roughly five million people in England and Wales and the vast majority of these lived in country districts and worked on the land. By 1815 the figure had more than doubled to about twelve million and most of the increase lived in towns and cities. By the end of the century England was becoming an urbanised or city-centred nation. Old established cities such as London and Bristol grew larger, while places like Manchester, Liverpool and Birmingham developed at an astonishing rate.

Manchester in 1770 had 30,000 inhabitants, 95,000 by 1801 and it could boast 238,000 in 1831. Oldham sprang from 300 in 1760 to 200,000 by the turn of the century. (Between 1776 and 1788 twenty-five cotton factories were built there.) London, then, as now, can be regarded as a special case. James I had written in one of his speeches to the Commons that 'with time England will be only London', for from 1500 to 1600 its population had increased five-fold to 250,000. By 1688 it was half a million; by 1800 a million, and today it is over eight millions.

The cause of this great increase in population is not easy to determine. It had taken over three centuries for the numbers to double, after the loss of life due to the Great Plague of 1348 (called the Black Death, during which between one-third and one-quarter of the nation was swept away). Partly the increase was due to better food, more medical attention and the growing prosperity of the country, especially as more people benefited from the first stages of industrialisation. It is more likely that the death rate went down, rather than the birth rate rose. The survival of more young children had the same effect as a rising birthrate would have done.

Behind this rapid growth in the size of towns and cities lie the great changes that took place in farming and industry at this time. The movements are known as Agricultural and Industrial Revolutions.

As the population rose, so it became more profitable for a farmer to increase the yield of his fields. The drive for greater efficiency caused the traditional ways of

The Effects of Enclosure

18 *Ducking punishment.* Even in the eighteenth century ducking the local scold (the bad-tempered housewife) or 'tell-tale' was a favourite diversion throughout Europe. This form of punishment probably stems from the trial by ordeal of water used in the early Middle Ages. Witches or people accused of sorcery were also ducked—often with fatal results.

farming, like the 'open-field' and 'strip' systems to give way before less wasteful methods. Land was enclosed or arranged into large fields which were hedged about and properly drained and ditched, so that the land was capable of producing more food than before. When new techniques of farming, like Jethro Tull's seed drill and 'Turnip' Townshend's Norfolk Rotation of Crops became widespread, these enclosed, modernised farms yielded good profits, especially to the larger landowners.

Like most attempts at modernising, however, the enclosure of land and the drive for efficiency and greater productivity brought some hardship in its wake. Thousands of small farmers and labourers, who had worked their strips or patches of land as their ancestors had done from medieval times, found themselves without a job. Many were evicted from their cottages and they wandered about the countryside looking for food and work. It is not surprising that these people, like the Elizabethan 'sturdy' beggars before them, should have become a great social menace, for many, of necessity, turned criminal and used both their wits and their brawn to keep themselves alive.

Growing centres like Birmingham and London were the places to which they turned, for there a man would have the chance to start on a different way of life; cotton mills in Bolton might need extra nimble hands, or John Wilkinson, ironmaster, might be taking on strong young men at a new iron-foundry in the Black Country. Not all the people who went to the towns were obliged to; many thought that anything was preferable to the old life of eking out a hard existence, tied to the soil, dependent upon the weather and the fillip of the occasional good harvest.

City Life Some went joyfully and full of ambition into the cities and readily adapted themselves to urban civilisation. Others were absorbed painlessly enough. To many, however, the transition from country to town proved too difficult. The hours of work were just as long, the conditions often atrocious, and there was the constant fear of losing one's job at the first hint of a trade depression. People found it hard to escape from the environment of factories and workshops, for most lived on top of their work in tiny houses, or in giant slums which resembled rabbit warrens.

In London, one family to a room was the usual housing for the poor, whilst the destitute were lucky to find a corner in a common lodging house. It was almost impossible to avoid rubbing shoulders with the pimps, prostitutes, thieves and murderers—the large class of desperate and depraved—which haunted the poorer areas. In the absence of a police force more efficient than the parish constable and the watch, these dregs of society were a constant menace to the law-abiding citizens. At the slightest provocation this section of the community, joined by numbers of men who were out of work, would terrorise the rest. The mob, so feared by the propertied classes, sometimes became associated with extreme and violent public opinion, especially in the 1760s when John Wilkes enjoined the mob's aid in his struggle against George III and his ministers.

Not until the nineteenth century did the working classes have the right to vote and, though a poor man was ostensibly equal before the law, he could seldom find the money to make this a reality. Often the only method open to him for the expression of grievances was the use of force. In time of high prices markets were

19 'Miseries of London': the coarseness and over-crowding of London, as depicted by Rowlandson. A street brawl such as this one between two drunken 'drabs' would often go uncontrolled. Few of the early police would dare to break up such a splendid entertainment.

ransacked and millers attacked. In Newcastle, in 1740, dissatisfied with the way the authorities were tackling the food scarcity, 'the Rabble then fell upon the Gentlemen in the Hall, wounded most of them, ransack'd the Place and the Court and Chambers, destroying the Public Writings and Accounts, and carried off nearly 1800L of the Town's Money. After this they patroll'd about the Streets, all the Shops being shut, and threatened to burn and destroy the Whole Place.' This sort of occurrence was by no means unique.

London

Many contemporaries considered the capital city the hub of the fashionable world and the centre of all the arts and amusements. 'When a man is tired of London he is tired of life', said the renowned eighteenth-century man of letters, Dr Samuel Johnson. The wealthy had elegant town houses built, designed to incorporate the best in architecture from Ancient Greece and Rome. Splendid balls and masquerades would be held in them and the upper classes spent much of their time visiting each other, leaving their cards and imbibing the most fashionable drink of the day—tea. This leisurely, cultured world of the upper-class is captured vividly by Alexander Pope in his poem *The Rape of the Lock*. He described the activity at Hampton Court under Queen Anne:

> *Here then, Great Anna, whom three Realms obey,*
> *Dost sometimes Counsel take, and sometimes tea.*

To others, though, such as Squire Weston in Henry Fielding's *Tom Jones*, London was a place where courtiers, and hangers-on, fops, beaux, swindlers and stock-exchange merchants, all joined forces to waste away the country's resources. Arthur Young in 1771 wrote that 'the debauched life of its inhabitants occasion them to be more idle than in the country'. He also bemoaned the fact that labourers were tempted to 'quit their healthy, clean fields for a region of stink, dirt and noise'. Once there, of course, they were soon fleeced of their valuables, and many descended into the criminal underworld.

There is some truth in the view that London was a malignant growth which sucked in good, wholesome people from outside and then treated them badly. In the first half of the eighteenth century most London parishes buried three people

33

for every two they baptised. Diseases, such as typhus and small-pox, took a heavy toll in the squalid and insanitary tenements into which much of London's population was packed.

Gin Drinking

Exceptional strength of character was needed if the inhabitants of the slums were to escape one of the worst evils of the eighteenth century, the addiction to spirits, to gin in particular. Gin was the easy way out, the anaesthetic and the temporary relief. Hogarth's print of Gin Lane bears grim testimony to the degradation which followed.

By 1722 there were nearly 7,000 dram shops in the cities of London and Westminster alone, besides all the gin that was sold off stalls and barrows in the street. Grocers, tobacconists and gaol-keepers sold it. Employers gave it as wages and mothers fed their babies on it to keep them quiet. Cheap as it was, the gin still had to be bought and the addicts could not drink and work. They sent their children out to steal or took to crime themselves. It was safer if their children did the stealing though, for there was no danger of parents being punished! The authorities recognised that gin-drinking was a major cause of disorder and crime among the labouring classes. Even employers showed anxiety. Walpole's Gin Act of 1736 tried to reduce the incidence of heavy drinking. A duty of 20s. a gallon was imposed and the cost of a licence to sell spirits was increased to £50. The main effect of these measures, however, was to increase disorder and troops had to be drafted in to London to suppress the rioting which ensued. Informers against those who contravened the act were beaten up by angry crowds and, without the aid of these spies upon whom the authorities leaned so heavily, the government allowed the measures to lapse. Eventually some measure of control was brought about by the 1751 Gin Act which prohibited the distillers from selling gin retail. The consumption fell from 8,495,000 gallons in 1751 to 2,100,000 gallons by 1760.

Most cities, especially the larger ones, were overcrowded, insanitary and poorly policed; in the eighteenth century they were the ideal breeding grounds for disease and disorder. Dr Johnson described London as a place 'where falling houses thunder on your head', and on more than one occasion he had to fight off a band of robbers with his stave. Even in the fashionable areas an important man was not always safe from attack; Members of Parliament would have escorts on their way home and most of the rich maintained a personal bodyguard. When the Duke of Bedford's tenants petitioned him to block up a certain unsavoury alley they said they were: 'continually disturbed by the dismal cry of Murder, and other disagreeable noises'. The literature of the period, such as novels like Defoe's *Moll Flanders* and Fielding's *Tom Jones*, is full of reference to the frightful conditions in which many of the city-dwellers lived.

Parish Constables

Few parish constables would venture into certain territories where a two-fingered whistle could summon up, as if from nowhere, a band of thugs only too willing to use their brawn and weapons against the forces of the law. The 'Charlies', had proved so ineffectual that they were objects of fun and pity. The parish constable was often the object of dislike—and his office was little sought-after. From the time

20 *'Gin Lane'*. This famous print by Hogarth shows the degradation which followed from drinking the cheap gin available in the early eighteenth century. The pawnbroker, the neglected children and the undertaker are prominently featured.

21 *The Charlie.* By the eighteenth century, in the fashionable parts of London the Charlie had his box at the end of the road (like a present-day sentry box)—where he could hide at the first sign of trouble. On many occasions Charlies were tipped over whilst asleep in their boxes.

of the Tudors theirs had been a thankless task. Their duties had included enforcing the magistrates' decisions on matters like eviction for rent arrears, flogging vagrants and clamping people in the stocks. In the seventeenth century constables had provoked hostility when called upon to enforce the licensing laws of James I. They had been required to flog offenders who failed to pay their fines within six days; and if they failed to administer the punishment or find someone else to do it, they had to go to prison themselves. Thus it was small wonder that the calibre of the men attracted to the post was very low.

The same was true, also, of their superiors, the justices of the peace and the magistrates. Petty justice was at a low level and far more so in the towns than in the country. In London, the 'trading Justice' (as he was often called), did a lucrative business out of fines and bribes; an income of £1,000 a year was possible. There were honest exceptions, but many actually conspired with thieves and receivers of stolen goods. Perhaps the quickest way to improve the standard of policing and petty justice would have been to pay the constables and magistrates a regular salary so that they could withstand bribes and attract good recruits; but this did not come until the turn of the nineteenth century.

In the absence of an efficient system of ensuring the peace and in face of the rising number of crimes the authorities relied increasingly on ferocious punishments to deter people. In 1688 the number of offences punishable by death was fifty but by the early nineteenth century the number had risen to 223. The prisons were full of wretches waiting to be hung for trivial offences like stealing a shilling or defacing Westminster Bridge; others were transported to the Colonies, first to America and then, after the War of Independence, to Australia. Often people would languish in gaol for years until, somehow, they managed to pay off their debts. Henry Fielding complained about the public executions, which were often on a large scale and to which crowds of spectators would flock. 'Many cartloads of our fellow creatures are once in six weeks . . . carried to slaughter'. Even so, a famous highwayman would be accorded the accolade of the crowd at his execution. The executioner needed to be thick-skinned, as the following extracts of the *Public Advertiser* show:

> *Wed. 20 April 1768.* Turlis, the Common Hangman, was much hurt and bruised by the mob throwing stones at the execution of three malefactors at Kingston.

> *Mon. 6 March 1769.* On Friday, a tradesman, convicted of wilful and corrupt perjury, stood in and upon the Pillory in High Street, Southwark, and was severely treated by the populace. They also pelted Turlis, the executioner, with stones and brick-bats, which cut him in the Head and Face in a terrible manner.

Alexander Pope questioned the humanity of the legal process in the couplet:

> Now hungry judges soon the sentence sign
> And wretches hang, that Jurymen may dine.

Despite the savage punishments—which were evidence enough of the greater incidence of crime and the failure to contain it—the eighteenth century was in many ways a golden age for the professional criminal. He stood little chance of being caught and if apprehended there were many ways of escaping the full rigours of the law. The hopeless inefficiency of the authorities and the general lawlessness of the early part of the eighteenth century is the background to the remarkable career of Jonathan Wild.

Jonathan Wild

Wild was one of many who were drawn to London to make their fortune. Prison was soon his lodging-house; but whilst there he mingled with all kinds of criminals, learned his craft and made his contacts. By 1712 he was running an empire of crime from Cripplegate. Among his many nefarious activities he blackmailed criminals and then accepted money from the courts when he eventually 'turned them in'. Because of this he achieved the name of 'Thief-taker General'. Besides this he made a reputation for himself by returning to the owners property which

22 *Jonathan Wild.* The most famous criminal in the eighteenth century is pelted by the mob as he goes to his execution at Tyburn in 1725. John Gay used the exploits of Jonathan Wild in his *Beggar's Opera,* a skit on Walpole, the leading Minister of the time.

had been stolen. At first he ingratiated himself by refusing payment for his public-spirited 'service', but soon his office became a kind of clearing house for 'lost' and stolen property. He was called in to return goods which he had bought cheaply from the thieves. Of course, before long he was planning the robberies himself and then returning the goods for a fee to the owners. Parliament legislated against this sort of trafficking of goods by the Act of 1717 which imposed fourteen years transportation for receiving stolen goods. Jonathan Wild, however, was as difficult to pin down as any twentieth-century Chicago gangster or 'hood'! In 1724 he was even petitioning to be made a Freeman of the City. Eventually, in 1725, he was caught and executed, amidst great excitement at Tyburn. He produced a document for the jury at his trial called 'A list of persons discovered apprehended and convicted of several robberies on the highway; also for burglary and housebreaking, and also for transportation by Jonathan Wild.' The list comprised the names of twenty-two housebreakers, thirty-five robbers, and ten return convicts whom he had caused to be hanged.

Much of the trouble was brought about by the questionable practice of giving rewards to informants. £40 was offered to people for securing the conviction of highway robbers, coiners and such, and this helped cause many an innocent victim or young person to be 'framed'. A favourite dodge was to induce a novice to join in a put-up robbery of an accomplice and then make sure he was caught. The money received from such a reward was called a 'blood-feast'! As usual the 'stool-pigeons' enjoyed the respect of neither the criminals nor the authorities.

The Secretary of State

The responsibility for the preservation of public order in the country was, at the government level, shared by the two Secretaries of State. These offices became increasingly important until the office of Home Secretary was evolved in 1782 to deal specifically with domestic affairs, and especially the maintenance of law and order. Included in their powers were those of authorising the arrest of suspects, searching private premises, seizing papers and documents and in time of acute crisis, the right to order out the militia and regular forces as the ultimate safeguard of public security.

Fortunately, the problem of maintaining internal order was not too serious a one in the eighteenth century. Except for the political conspiracy and uprisings connected with the 1715 and 1745 Jacobite rebellions, there were few popular outbreaks of disorder on a large scale with political aims. Disturbances tended to be local ones, connected usually with scarcity and high prices and with changes in the taxation system. The labourer swelled the ranks of the mob over Walpole's Excise scheme of 1733, when a levy on the consumption of wine and tobacco was attempted. People were goaded into violent protest over abuses arising from the

23 An execution outside Newgate Prison, from a drawing by Rowlandson. Notice the holiday atmosphere, food-sellers doing a good trade and the well-to-do person enjoying an excellent gallows-side seat in his own sedan chair.

press-gang or amid the general and often drunken excitement which frequently attended elections for parliamentary candidates. It was the duty of the local magistrate to suppress disorder and the ancient system of force supplied by an unpaid local constabulary usually proved inadequate; the local militia and, on many occasions, regular troops had to be called in to restore order.

The law against rioting offences was severe; it could be treated as treason. By the Riot Act of 1715 an assembly of twelve or more people threatening the public peace had, on pain of conviction, to disperse within an hour, when ordered to do so by a magistrate. But there was some doubt about whether force could be used if the magistrate had failed to read the 'riot Act'. During the pro-Wilkes riots in 1769 a criminal indictment was lodged against a soldier who had killed one of the mob attempting to set Wilkes free from gaol. Hence the authorities were loathe to use military force to keep order. When Lord George Gordon and a mass of petitioners against the Catholic Relief Bill of 1778 marched to the Commons in June, 1780, ugly scenes of violence occurred. The poor and the lawless found in the anti-government and anti-Catholic demonstrations an excellent opportunity to give vent to their hatred of the rich. Property was destroyed, Roman Catholic chapels attacked. Five rioters were committed to Newgate Prison; the mob then set it on fire and let all the prisoners out. The following day Fleet Prison was attacked and an attempt was even made at storming the Bank of England. Firm military action was lacking, until George III prevailed on the Privy Council to give the necessary orders for troops to be summoned to restore order and the Guards were posted at the Bank where they exercised the same duties as they do to this day.

Many of the people who stood trial for their part in the rioting turned out to be hitherto respectable working men. After this, any open demonstration by the working classes were immediately regarded as tantamount to revolution, especially after the full horrors of the French Revolution became known in the 1790s. Government officials also were turning over in their minds the possibility of keeping order without the use of military force and proposals were mooted for the establishment of a regular, salaried police force.

By the end of the eighteenth century then, crime and disorder were increasing and the traditional methods of keeping the peace were patently inadequate. The population increase, together with the rapid growth of towns during the early stages of the Industrial Revolution, caused the authorities to examine closely and put more money into the promising experiments which had been started in the mid-eighteenth century—the pioneering efforts of the Bow Street Runners.

The growth of the police force from the City of Westminster and the men who made it possible is the subject of the next chapter.

Further Reading   Frederick J. Lyons, *Jonathan Wilde Prince of Robbers* (M. Joseph 1936)
Daniel Defoe, *Moll Flanders* (Pan Books)

4 Makers of the Police—The Fore-runners

Fourteen years after Jonathan Wild was hanged at Tyburn, Colonel de Veil opened his 'public office' in Bow Street. He was an unusually zealous magistrate for his time, and as a Justice of the Peace for Westminster he showed great courage in the way he handled mobs. Bow Street was an area with a bad reputation and de Veil found himself very hard-worked. He was followed shortly afterwards by another remarkable man, Henry Fielding, in 1748.

When Fielding took up office in Bow Street he had no regular salary; just as prison governors made the post pay by charging their prisoners for lodging, so a magistrate was expected to make what he could out of the imposition of fines. The constable also lined his pocket by accepting bribes and letting malefactors go free. It was by no means uncommon for innocent people to be arrested for trivial offences in the hope that they would prefer to pay a small sum to avoid a night's sojourn in prison. A similar system was often worked by the 'Charlies'. Thus, at the street level the law was riddled with bribery.

Henry Fielding (1707–54)

Henry Fielding was exceptional. 'Soon', he wrote, 'I had reduced an income of the dirtiest money on earth to little more than £300 and of this my clerk took his share.' At the time he became magistrate he was just finishing his novel *Tom Jones*

24 *Henry Fielding,* novelist and magistrate, who founded the Bow Street Runners.

25 *Townshend,* the most famous of the Bow Street runners became both the scourge of the underworld and the envy of many of his contemporaries, largely because he was on speaking terms with King George III.

and was in debt; his obvious honesty is thus even more noteworthy. In 1743 he wrote an ironic novel, *The Life of the Late Jonathan Wild the Great.* He was keen and took his post seriously. Because of an increase in rioting and crime during the forties, Fielding produced *An Enquiry into the Cause of Robberies, etc.* in January, 1751. His proposals so interested the authorities that funds were made available for him to set up a small force of constables specially picked for reliability (all but one were trusted ex-constables of Westminster). Most important, however, was the fact that they were paid a salary high enough for them to be able to withstand bribes. They formed, in effect, the first detective force in England.

From the start, 'Mr Fielding's People' as they were called, were very successful, partly no doubt because at first they wore no uniform. Later they became known as 'Runners' and then unpopularly were called 'Thief-takers' because some of their methods were reminiscent of Jonathan Wild; they maintained close contact with the criminal underworld. Henry Fielding died in 1754 and he was succeeded by his brother John, who was blind. He made famous the name of the Bow Street

Runners or 'Robin Redbreasts' as they were later called (from the scarlet waist-coats they wore under their frock-coats). The government was persuaded to continue to provide funds for the force, and besides the uniform the men were supplied with a small, wooden hollow baton called a 'tip-staff' which was used mainly as a weapon but also on occasion for carrying a warrant of arrest. A pair of handcuffs and a pistol completed the equipment.

Small in numbers though the force was, it rapidly became feared by the criminals. The Runners received a regular wage of a guinea a week on which they could exist comfortably. Their services could also be hired for a guinea a day, plus expenses up to 14s., and so great was the demand for their expert help, that they travelled all over the country, solving robberies, protecting jewels and so on. Several of the early Runners like Sayer, Vickeray and Ruthven became well-known, but the most famous was Townshend, who proved a favourite in court circles, guarding the plate at official functions and keeping out undesirables.

26 John Wilkes, M.P. for Aylesbury, brought great pressure to bear on the government in the 1760s. In editions 17 and 45 of his newspaper *The North Briton* he attacked the policies of George III. He was arrested and during his campaign to win justice in the courts he and his supporters made skilful use of the London mob. Under the banners of 'Liberty' they rioted almost uncontrollably and on one occasion Wilkes was rescued by the mob as the law officers were taking him to prison. Wilkes could never have exerted so much influence if an efficient police force had been at hand to check the rioting.

The banks also made use of their services. When they had been robbed they were usually more concerned with recovering the money than with apprehending the thieves. In fact bank officials were prepared to make a deal with robbers and decline to prosecute. The Runners, with their specialist knowledge of the underworld, would be brought in as go-betweens. This partly explains why the Runners were smeared with the charge of being 'Thief-takers' in the Jonathan Wild tradition.

During the sixties, John Wilkes made skilful use of the mob in London. As part of his campaign against what he called the tyranny of Parliament and the King's Ministers, demonstrations and marches were organised. Banners bearing such slogans as 'Wilkes and Liberty' were paraded and pro-Wilkes societies were formed in many of the large cities. His campaign against authority attracted many sincere adherents; it also gave the discontented lower classes an opportunity to riot and pillage. When the mob was out in force no constable would be seen and troops would have to be used to restore order. The St George's Fields Massacre in 1768, in which six people were killed and twenty injured, caused widespread alarm. The troops had feared an attempt to rescue Wilkes from custody. Crime also was on the increase and throughout the sixties considerable social distress had given rise to food riots and general lawlessness; all this combined to make Parliament set up a Committee in 1770 to inquire into the recent increase in crime and lawlessness and to consider more effective preventive measures.

Sir John Fielding was asked for his views and one of the reforms he advocated was the improvement of prison conditions—at that time first offenders and even innocent people were put in custody along with hardened and vicious criminals. He also questioned the deterrent effect of the savage punishments which were imposed by the courts. He argued that the best way of preventing crime was to extend the Bow Street system. Most of his reforms were too prophetic and too expensive to put into operation, but one idea he did put into effect straightaway was the production of a regular police bulletin. In 1771 a murder in Chelsea gave him the chance to launch his scheme. Hand-bills were printed with details of the men wanted for questioning and copies were sent—by horse—to every postmaster in the country, even to Edinburgh and Dublin.

A £50 reward was offered for information leading to a conviction. The criminals were duly caught and this system proved so encouraging that a Quarterly Pursuit and then a Weekly Pursuit was produced. In 1786 the first number of 'Public Hue and Cry' came out and details of crimes, wanted men and rewards were posted all over the country for people to read. Provincial authorities welcomed this means 'of intercourse between the civil power in the country and in the metropolis', but, though Bow Street was achieving renown in the fight against crime, there was no central police authority powerful enough to enforce a common set of regulations. The government was fast becoming aware of the need for one—the Gordon Riots of 1780 had emphasised the inability of those in charge of civil power to maintain public order. As John Fielding lay dying in 1780 his Chief Police Office in Bow Street was wrecked; Newgate Prison was stormed, fired and gutted; and the Old Bailey, King's Bench Prison and Fleet Prison were all damaged.

Responsible public opinion was emphatic that this kind of disorder should not

27 *The Gordon Riots, 1780.* Lord George Gordon led anti-Catholic demonstrations in London. This started several days of ugly rioting until the militia restored order. Here is a contemporary impression of the burning of Newgate Prison.

be allowed to recur. The *Public Advertiser* of 14 June 1780 expressed the general view of the authorities and the public. 'The late riots were shocking in their effects, but should a vigilant and regular police force be established, nothing of this kind can happen in the future.' But as soon as order was restored, nothing was done on a national or large scale to set up an efficient system of policing the country. Still too many people thought that a powerful police force would lead to the diminution of personal liberties. In any case, it would have been a costly business and a government's duty was to keep expenditure down. As it happened, after the French Revolution in 1789, Pitt the Younger and his government produced repressive legislation in order to maintain internal law and order. There was a genuine fear that radical working-class movements and trade unions of workers were being urged into revolutionary activities by the French. The Habeas Corpus Act (the right of trial soon after being arrested) was suspended in 1794. In 1799 'Combination' Acts forbade workmen to campaign together for higher wages and better conditions. Despite widespread acquiescence in these harsh measures (for England was after all at war with France), it is doubtful whether the country would have entertained kindly the idea of any form of national force for keeping order. In fact a government-directed police force would have echoed Cromwellian military rule, and smacked of Jacobinism and the armed terror of the Revolution. People were in any case extremely sceptical that a group of civilians would be able to control and prevent riots; even military forces had found it difficult, as the Wilkes and Gordon riots had shown.

There were signs, however, by the end of the eighteenth century, that some progress was being made. Bow Street under Sampson Wright had, in addition to a

45

small force of Thief-takers, a Foot Patrole of sixty-eight men armed with cutlasses, ununiformed and paid on a part-time basis of half-a-crown per night (captains— five shillings). Dublin in 1786 adopted some of the provisions of a rejected police bill of Pitt the Younger and set up three paid 'Commissioners' and a small paid constabulary. A breakthrough came in England when in 1792 the Middlesex Justices Police Bill appointed seven Public Offices in the metropolis, each with three magistrates. All were salaried at £400 per annum and each office had a small force of paid police officers, generally six, for an experimental three-years period. This system was made permanent in 1812.

Patrick
Colquhoun
(1745–1820)
Out of interest in the problems of the poor and the lawlessness in London during the closing years of the eighteenth century, Colquhoun found himself involved with advocating reforms. His *Treatise of the Policing of the Metropolis* proposed, in effect, what Peel was to create a generation later.

> 1. A central board of salaried Police Commissioners were to be given wide powers in every part of the capital and they were to be responsible only to the Home Department. Under them would be superintending officers controlling a district served by a Police Office. Each superintendent would command an increased force of police.
>
> 2. A reserve force of police was advocated enrolled from a reformed and carefully selected watch. These would receive good pay and be eligible for promotion to the regular police.
>
> 3. The City of London was included in the scheme and also provisions were made for financing this police force. He proposed various licences for street dealers.

Colquhoun's treatise caused a big outcry from the vested interests in Parliament, especially from the M.P.s representing the City and the bill to implement his proposals was dropped. However, he was directly responsible for the founding of the River Police. In this Treatise he had written of the crime which was rampant in the London Docks, where 'lumpers', 'glutmen' and 'scuffle-hunters', with juvenile 'mud-larks' helped to pillage the ships and warehouses. Receivers organised the thefts and they were often aided by ships' officers. In 1798 the Marine Police headquarters was established at Wapping New Stairs, with a permanent staff of eighty men. 1800 saw the passing of the Thames Police Bill, proposed by Jeremy Bentham and Patrick Colquhoun, which authorised three magistrates and a number of permanent police to help check the crime and disorder connected with the river traffic. Only because Bentham and Colquhoun had convinced the authorities that money would be saved by these measures, did they in fact go forward. The drop in the volume of thefts soon more than paid for the upkeep of the river police force.

Whilst the River Police was proving a success, Bow Street under Richard Ford, the chief magistrate in the early years of the nineteenth century, was developing a campaign against highwaymen. In 1763 George Grenville, First Lord of the Treasury, had sanctioned the cost of a 'Horse Patrole' of eight men to combat the

28 *'Malefactors go to their Execution',* (from a cartoon by Rowlandson)—and provide a suitable moral warning for the young. The coffin is big enough for all three.

daring robberies of highwaymen on the outskirts of London, but this scheme had been abandoned after eighteen months, on the grounds of expense. In 1805 the growing incidence of robberies caused the Mounted Patrol to be reconstituted. A force of fifty-two men and two inspectors patrolled the main roads in shifts, calling out 'Bow Street Patrole' to passers-by. The cost of this was over £5,000 a year (each man earned 5s. per night) but the rapid decline in robbery on the highway again justified the expense. Their uniform consisted of:

Black leather hat	Blue greatcoat	Scarlet waistcoat
Leather stock	Blue trousers	beneath greatcoat
White leather gloves	Riding boots with steel spurs	Sabre, pistol, truncheon and a pair of handcuffs

Sensible as these arrangements were, they only scratched at the surface. It must have reassured scared travellers to be greeted occasionally by the call of 'Bow Street Patrole', but people were far from safe, even in their own beds. In 1811 a series of horrible murders by a John Williams in Ratcliffe Highway, Shadwell, caused great consternation in London. The average citizen felt unsafe and great pressure was applied for improved security arrangements. Schemes were again set up, but again they were shelved.

On the evidence submitted to Parliament in 1812 there was one watchman to *'Charlies'* every seventy-eight houses. They were paid between £13 and £26 per year but few who applied for the job were fit to do it properly. The *Morning Herald* of 30 October 1802 gives an insight into what the public thought of the post of watchman:

> A man who presented himself for the office of watchman to a parish at the West End of the Town very much infested by depredators, was lately turned away from the Vestry with this reprimand: 'I am astonished at the impudence of such a great sturdy, strong fellow as you are, being so idle as to apply for a watchman's situation when you are capable of labour.'

47

Another contemporary said, 'The London Watch is to all intents and purposes a complete humbug of the first water.' Clearly, there was not much esteem attaching to the post! In fact, the 'Charlies' almost since their inception had been a standing joke. John Parsons in 1827 recounted: 'A friend of mine couldn't sleep at all. His physicians put him on an experiment. They dressed him in a watchman's coat, put a lantern in his hand, and placed him in a sentry-box and in ten minutes he was asleep.'

Parliamentary Concern

Eventually, after the end of the wars against Napoleon, the Government set up yet another Committee (in 1816) to inquire into the causes of crime in the metropolis, the conduct of magistrates and those in charge of policing duties. The inquiry dragged on for four years and lasted through a period which was perhaps the most troubled in the nineteenth century. The post-war years were full of violent disorder and one might have expected strong recommendations to emerge from the deliberations.

The Committee, though slow to formulate a report, was thorough. Evidence was gathered from all sides. Sayer and Townshend, the Bow Street Runners, were interviewed and they maintained that a guinea a week was too low a salary for the police—it helped cause dishonesty. The Runners also condemned the practice of giving rewards, for this encouraged the police to make frequent convictions—often to obtain a share in the 'Blood Money'. Shortly afterwards a Bow Street Runner called George Vaughan was discovered in this malpractice and sentenced to be transported! Other evidence from them included graphic descriptions of the hazard they had faced in their policing careers; how they had to walk in fives in certain places like Chick Lane, Black Boy Alley and Field Lane (where the Artful Dodger

29 The pillory. As there were over 200 offences carrying the death sentence, public humiliation of the type shown below (1807) was for minor offences.

was instructed by Fagin, the Jew). A member of the London Military Association described the haunts of criminals for the benefit of the committee:

> The houses are divided, from top to bottom, into many compartments, with doors of communication to each, and also with the adjacent houses some have two, others three, others four, doors opening into different alleys. To such a height is our neglect of police arrived, the owners of these houses make no secret of their being kept for the entertainment of thieves. In many rooms I saw six, seven, eight or ten men in bed without shirts, all pictures of misery. Into one loft we crept through a trap-door, our bayonets and pistols in our hands. . . . We were inclined to think we were often in the haunts of highwaymen as well as of infantry thieves, for in some places we found the bones of horses.

Eventually, the report was published in 1822, and much of it consisted of a detailed survey of the existing framework for keeping order. The separate police establishments for each parish were noted, comprising as they usually did: a high constable, a beadle, several petty constables, watchmen and street-keepers (whose chief duties were to remove nuisances and arrest vagrants). The separate police forces of the metropolis, those of the City and the Bow Street establishment, were mentioned and the recent success of the Horse Patrole came in for commendation.

Nothing new was said when the inefficiency of the parish constables and watchmen was contrasted with the efficiency of the City and Bow Street organisations. Nor did the Committee break fresh ground with the information that each parish acted independently and that a constable could arrest only in his own parish. Even the final recommendation had been mooted before—that there should be set up a single police force for the whole of the metropolis. Colquhoun had proposed this twenty years earlier.

These measures for improving the policing of the metropolis seemed obvious, but at least they were now fully agreed upon by the committee set up by Parliament. It was to take another seven years, however, before they could be put into operation by Peel.

Further Reading

B. M. Jones, *Henry Fielding, Novelist and Magistrate* (Allen & Unwin 1938)
Dorothy George, *London Life in the Eighteenth Century* (Kegan Paul 1925)
Raymond Postgate, *That Devil Wilkes* (Constable & Co. 1930)
Peter Quennell, *Hogarth's Progress* (Collins 1955)

5 Peel and the Reform of the Penal Code

The first two decades of the nineteenth century were not happy years either for the bulk of the population or for the government. Enough problems and hardship were caused by the war with Napoleon; even the end of the war in 1815 brought few of the sweet fruits of victory. Indeed, the years from 1815 to 1820 can be described as the worst in the nineteenth century, in terms of widespread disorder, dissatisfaction with authority, and hunger. Many historians see in this period the closest thing to revolution and overturning of government that had been witnessed since 1688 and the abdication of James II.

Some of the trouble can be ascribed to the natural difficulty of readjustment to peace-time conditions after twenty years of warfare against France. High unemployment, heavy taxation, dislocation of trade and the demobilisation of soldiers and sailors (about 200,000 of them) all contributed to distress. Until the manufacturers could get back to normal peace-time production and more stable prices, the working classes were bound to feel the pinch.

The natural after-effects of war only partly explain the disorder of the period. To Karl Marx studying in London in the 1840s the real trouble stemmed from the fact that by the 1820s the industrialisation of society had caused more power and wealth to fall into the hands of the capitalists, the financiers and manufacturers. The factory workers on the other hand were worse off than ever; a great gulf existed between the rich and the poor which was getting wider. The cotton worker was becoming both a slave to his machine and its owner (a mere mill 'hand') and the first dispensable victim of the trade cycle. There was a considerable amount of truth in this type of argument when this particular period is closely examined. Even the Corn Laws of 1815 which kept up the price of corn, and hence bread, were largely introduced to aid the landowners and especially the country gentry. When income-tax was abolished at the end of the war, revenue was raised by increased duties on everyday consumer goods like tea, beer, tobacco and soap and it seemed that the poor were being taxed rather than the rich. The Game Laws also reflected the spirit of the times. It was legal for land owners to set iron man-traps to catch poachers just as they would a wild animal and heavy penalties were imposed on any man found trying to supplement his meagre diet.

If, as many Victorians such as Benjamin Disraeli maintained, England was fast becoming two nations, that of the rich and the poor, Parliament seemed solidly behind the ranks of the wealthy. William Pitt's repressive legislation during the 1790s, imposed in a time of national emergency, was continued in the years following the victory of Waterloo. Lord Liverpool's government maintained, with some justification, that the emergency had not disappeared. There was the danger of internal revolution to be overcome, and he used a peace-time army of 25,000 men to help maintain order. When the Duke of Wellington joined the cabinet in 1818 it seemed as if the military was about to take over. The government had, in fact, relied increasingly on the army to maintain internal order once it was obvious that the civil authorities had no hope of doing so. This was brought home very clearly when in 1811 the machine-breakers known as 'Luddites' became a law unto themselves in the Midlands.

The Luddites

This secret organisation, led, it was said by Ned Ludd, or 'King Ludd' from Sherwood Forest, made systematic, well-organised raids on the 'wide-frame' stocking machines which were causing unemployment and falling wages in the industry. Throughout the late eighteenth century, angry mobs would occasionally vent their hatred on the machines which appeared to be taking away their means of livelihood. In 1800 the earnings of the hand-loom weaver was approximately 27s. a week; by 1815 about 15s; and by the early twenties little more than 8s. a week. Some expression of resentment was only to be expected.

However, the Luddite riots were quite exceptional. Throughout Nottinghamshire, and then later in Lancashire and Cheshire, well-disciplined gangs smashed up machinery in scores of small towns and villages. Within a year over a thousand machines were smashed. The machine-breakers struck rapidly under cover of darkness, and so ineffective in coping were the traditional forces of law and order that central government enacted special legislation. At the Nottingham Assizes of March 1812, seven Luddites were sentenced to transportation for life. Soon after, William Cartwright's mill near Huddersfield was attacked at midnight, but the mill owner and several soldiers beat off an attack of some one hundred and fifty machine-breakers, killing two of them. Within a year, fourteen of the assailants

30 *The poacher up before the beak.* The Game Laws of 1816 pressed heavily on country-dwellers. A poacher was liable to transportation or worse. This print shows the wife and child of a poacher pleading for mercy in the local magistrate's house.

31 *Jeremiah Brandeth*, the Nottingham Captain. He led the Derbyshire rising of 1817 which Sidmouth, the Home Secretary, feared was part of a widespread revolt centred on the Midlands and the North. With a small army of unemployed textile workers Brandeth set out to capture Nottingham Castle but Oliver the Spy had played him false. He was captured and hanged with three of his henchmen. Fourteen men were transported.

were hanged for their part in the affair. The Home Secretary, Lord Sidmouth, thought that these hangings would have 'the happiest effects in various parts of the kingdom'. Certainly 1813 was much less violent; the 1,200 regular troops stationed in the Northern and Midland counties were gradually withdrawn from their policing duties. Sporadic outbreaks of machine-wrecking continued to disturb the industrial towns, however, for several years to come. Some of the frame-breakers went on strike—8,000 of them in 1817—in an attempt to secure a Bill against 'cut-ups' (cheap stockings which flooded the market); others continued to pin their faith on violent action. Such a man was Jeremiah Brandeth, 'The Nottingham Captain', who led the Derbyshire Rising in 1817.

The Luddite, machine-breaking movement, was entirely an economic affair; few wreckers had any intention of overturning the government or advocating a political reform programme. Other movements, though, were considered dangerous to the government. At this time many radical societies were formed to give expression to various grievances like low wages, the Corn Laws, harsh factory conditions, and some of them advocated a reform of the franchise; a vote for all men being a preliminary to all other reform. Agitations and public meetings caused the authorities great anxiety, even though most of the leaders of the radicals, people like William Cobbett and 'Orator' Hunt advocated peaceful methods of gaining their aims.

Much of the disorder and animosity of the lower classes towards the government of this period can be directly ascribed to the methods used for keeping the peace. When force, in the form of military swords was used, harmonious relationships were unlikely to prevail. But even in these troubled years few people subscribed to the idea of a professional police force, trained, controlled and paid for by local authorities, from local taxation. Even after the shocking murders in London in 1811 had caused widespread anxiety, many people thought as did J. W. Ward, who wrote: 'They have an admirable police at Paris, but they pay for it dear enough. I had rather half-a-dozen people's throats were cut in Ratcliffe Highway every three or four years than be subject to domiciliary visits, spies, and all the rest of Fouché's contrivances.'

Why did any form of realistic policing cause such animosity? Partly it was due to the prevailing attitude that freedom would be severely curtailed—the eighteenth-century philosophy had been that government should be as unobtrusive as possible. But mostly it was because the existing practices seemed tyrannical enough—any extension of these methods were likely to produce even more tyranny. What, then, were the methods used for ensuring internal order?

The Peace-keeping System

The Home Office was at the head of the system, under the recently created office of Home Secretary (evolved from one of the two Secretaries of State). Lord Sidmouth took over at the Home Office in 1812. To him and his officials all kinds of information were fed from various parts of the country—from magistrates, manufacturers, informers and police-agents. Secret agents were employed by the Home Secretary, usually men of dubious character, who travelled the country hunting out potentially dangerous societies and groups. They infiltrated into seditious societies, and men like Oliver the 'Spy' were known even to foster trouble so that they could report it in good time to the authorities. These agents were untrained and unreliable but they were necessary for effective action by the government, who could be forewarned of impending disturbances and certainly became forearmed. For the Home Secretary kept in close touch with the heads of the armed forces.

Little of the peace-keeping machinery had changed in over three hundred years, and, except for the semi-official police force in London, the rest was amateur, unpaid and voluntary. The bulk of the responsibility still rested, as it had done from the time of the Tudors and even before, on the landed gentry and the services of ordinary citizens. Without the able and enthusiastic aid of the Lord Lieutenants of the counties, the justices of the peace and the self-organised citizens of the towns, the Home Office and the Government of the day would have been at best ineffective, and at worst compelled to resort to military rule.

This, to some extent, the Government was obliged to do in the decade 1810–20. The Lord Lieutenant had the power to call out the yeomanry and the militia and this was used to good effect by the Dukes of Newcastle and Rutland in the Luddite areas of Nottinghamshire and Leicestershire. Even the justices of the peace frequently employed their power to call out the militia to disperse mobs or check disorder. Some were overzealous but many were apathetic. In any case the efficiency of the justice of the peace in the urban areas was considerably governed by whether the town had a corporation or not. Places like Manchester, Bolton and Stockport had no corporate body and hence no centre from which to organise the defence of property, the regular levy of taxes to pay for policing expenses and the regular supply of man-power for special duty.

Nottingham showed what could be done with the full help of a corporation. During the worst Luddite period, 1811–12, the town possessed a body of regular, efficient paid police and a well-organised system of Watch and Ward. Many of the citizens made up a large body of special constables. Lying right in the heart of 'Ned Ludd' country, Nottingham managed to keep the machine-breakers under control. But even this town had to call in the assistance of regular troops on occasion. In the summer of 1817 though, they were ready for the attack on Nottingham Castle by unemployed textile workers led by Jeremiah Brandeth. Oliver the Spy had promised Brandeth that other contingents would join in the attack but all they were met by was the party of troops ready and waiting to capture the marchers

Brandeth and three others were hanged and fourteen transported, whilst many more were imprisoned.

In London, the Spa Fields meetings of 1816 caused the Government great alarm. Two huge rival assemblies advocating reform, one of which was led by the Radicals and addressed by 'Orator' Hunt, ended with the London mob getting out of hand. The authorities, fearful of more riots, suspended Habeas Corpus again and passed further laws against seditious meetings. When in 1817 the Manchester unemployed planned a great march to London, where they hoped to petition the regent for the reform of parliament, the relief of distress and the cancellation of Sidmouth's recent measures, the authorities were firm. A big send-off in St Peter's Fields, Manchester, was planned for the 'blanketeers', as they were called (for they planned to carry blankets for the journey). But the march never really got under way. Troops broke up the meeting and arrested the leaders. Many of the crowd were arrested as vagrants and spent some time in prison without trial—then possible after the government had suspended Habeas Corpus.

So when in August, 1819, a monster meeting to advocate for reform and relief was planned in the same St Peter's Fields, more trouble was expected.

32 The 'Massacre of Peterloo', Manchester 1819. When it became known that innocent women and children had died at the hands of the Manchester Yeomanry, there was a great outcry against the government. The use of the militia to control meetings of this sort came under more criticism. Liverpool, however, supported the actions of the local magistrates and the Six Acts were rushed through Parliament to restrict political meetings.

33 *The Cato Street Conspiracy, February 1820.* Arthur Thistlewood, who had been imprisoned for challenging Sidmouth to a duel, planned to blow up the entire Cabinet. The government got wind of this and publicised a 'Grand Cabinet Dinner' which was to be held. The conspirators fell into the trap, were caught and executed. The scene above was described by Ruthven, the famous Bow Street Runner.

About fifty thousand men and women from all over Lancashire trooped into Manchester to hear 'Orator' Hunt. Most were dressed in their Sunday clothes and they carried banners calling for annual parliaments and universal suffrage ('one man, one vote'). The remarkable thing was that the processions were so orderly. Women and children were there, as part of the proceedings, and this was to ensure only the most peaceable of meetings. And it proved peaceful until the magistrates used the Manchester Yeomanry, a volunteer body of cavalry, to arrest 'Orator' Hunt once he had started talking. In such a throng, a woman was knocked down and her child killed and before long the Yeomanry had to be rescued at sword point by the regular cavalry, the 15th Hussars, again on the orders of the magistrate, Mr Hulton. By the time the crowd had been dispersed eleven were dead, including two women and some four hundred seriously injured. Immediately, the event was christened 'The Massacre of Peterloo', in reference to the glorious victory of Waterloo four years before. It was a sign of contempt for the 'victory' of the magistrates, who nevertheless received full backing from Liverpool's government.

Then Sidmouth rushed through Parliament the Six Acts, which extended the laws relating to public order and severely curtailed the freedom of manoeuvre of movements like that of the Radicals.

Of the Six Acts the most stringent clauses were that meetings for the presenta-

'Massacre of Peterloo'

34 Duelling. Whereas the two 'drabs' of the London streets fought tooth and nail before a huge crowd, gentlemen often settled their differences with duelling pistols, with no audience other than their 'seconds' and a referee. Normally the duelling grounds were on the outskirts of the cities for duelling was illegal.

tion of petitions were limited to the residents of the parish in which the meeting was held—thus large crowds were made illegal. A stamp tax was extended from newspapers to all periodical pamphlets of a certain size. This was aimed at radical literature such as William Cobbett's *Register*. Magistrates were given wide powers of search for blasphemous or seditious literature.

The government was understandably unpopular and a change to a less repressive attitude might have come about more quickly if it had not been for an ill-conceived plot to blow up the entire Cabinet and then seize London. This scheme, called the Cato Street Conspiracy, was the brain-child of Arthur Thistlewood, and was easily foiled, for it was in fact in part engineered by government spies. The ring-leaders were caught and executed. Thistlewood was the last person in England to be beheaded. Lord Liverpool's government used this plot to advantage, making the most of the supposed existing danger to authority.

By 1820, then, when the Parliamentary Committee was finishing its deliberations on the need for better policing of the metropolis, the use of military force to maintain order had proved most inefficient. If the troops obeyed orders and fired, the result was civilian bloodshed and popular outcry; if they sympathised at all with the mob, as they had done on occasion during the Wilkes riots, then the government was helpless. When in 1820 there was a threat of mutiny amongst the 300 Guards on whom London's public safety ultimately depended, more and more responsible citizens thought of alternative protection. The Duke of Wellington wrote to Lord Liverpool at this time: 'In my opinion the Government ought, without loss of a moment's time, to adopt measures to form either a police in London or military corps, which should be of a different description from the regular military force, or both.'

It was Wellington who had created a new police force in Ireland, which Robert Peel as Chief Secretary in Ireland from 1812 to 1818 had improved. These two then took up the cause of police reform in England and their efforts culminated in the formation of the Metropolitan Police Force in 1829.

Sir Robert Peel,
1788–1850

Robert Peel took over as Home Secretary from Lord Sidmouth in 1822 and he was to hold this important office, with only one break, up to 1830. His great achievement during this time was that he made the English Common Law more humane and efficient. When men could still be executed for such trivial offences as impersonating a Chelsea Pensioner or defacing Westminster Bridge and over two hundred crimes carried the death penalty, juries were reluctant to find men guilty and send them to the gallows. Sir Samuel Romilly had for years collected masses of evidence in his efforts to persuade Parliament to reform the penal code and he eventually secured the removal of pick-pocketing from the list of capital offences. Sir James Mackintosh, John Howard, Elizabeth Fry and many others had launched campaigns for the improvement of prison conditions and of the penal system (see chapter 6). Peel followed up these pioneer efforts by getting over a hundred offences removed from the list of those punishable by death. He also was instrumental in improving the state of the larger prisons: the vicious practice of the payment of gaolers' fees was forbidden, most prisons were to be inspected and women prisoners guarded by female warders. But no other Home Secretary followed up Peel's work for many years. The state of the smaller prisons continued to be disgraceful and Charles Dickens was able to write so scathingly of debtors' prisons from family experience—his father had twice been incarcerated for debt.

Peel could only justify 'softening up' the law and the removal of numerous capital offences, by ensuring that the criminal was more readily apprehended, and that there was more certainty of punishment. (The increase of savage penalties during the eighteenth century showed only too well that few criminals were being caught.) By 1826 Peel was moving towards the idea of a central authority to organise both the prevention of crime and the apprehension of those who broke the law. Knowing the strength of self-government in the City of London, and perhaps remembering the outcry against Colquhoun's proposals twenty years before, he decided to leave the City out of his proposals. 'I should be afraid to meddle with it,' he said. If he had to tread warily in the case of the City of London, the climate of opinion in the country as a whole was more favourable. Back in 1820, after the disturbances and riots over the question of which route should be taken by Queen

35 The Burning of Bristol, 1831. When the Lords rejected the Great Reform Bill in October 1831 widespread demonstrations occurred. There were riots in the Midlands, and at Bristol the Tory M.P. was attacked, the Mansion House was sacked and the Bishop's Palace was burnt. The cavalry eventually restored order.

36 Regency 'Bucks'. Out on a drunken revel the 'bucks' find themselves fighting to evade arrest from the Charlies and their helpers. This is the age of Beau Brummel as can be seen from the dress of the man with the text-book straight-left.

Caroline's coffin this extract had appeared in *The Times*:

> If the civil power were increased, as it ought to be, in strength, there would be no pretext for the employment of soldiers in their modern and extraordinary character of policemen. Fifty police officers on horseback would in point of mere efficiency, be worth a whole regiment of dragoons. If none but the civil power appeared, there is not a decent individual among the King's subjects who would not eagerly assist them, in the suppression of a riot, and in bringing the abettors of it to punishment.

(This can be compared with the recent exhortation by the police to 'Have a go' at bank-robbers and such criminals—in fact to assist the police in the execution of their duties.)

By 1828 Peel, a very sensible and cautious reformer, was able to say: 'The time is come when . . . we may fairly pronounce that the country has outgrown her police institutions, and that the cheapest and safest course will be found in the introduction of a new mode of protection.'

When eventually Peel cautiously put his bill before Parliament he had decided to make a complete break with the past; the relics of the past, the patrols, Runners, watchmen, parish constables and beadles—all would have to go if there was to be a genuine and efficient force of police in the metropolis. The force was to be under semi-military discipline, with uniform dress for each rank and commanded by a central office whose orders would be obeyed in all districts of London outside the city.

In 1829, he proposed in parliament the establishment, under the Home Secretary, of a controlling central office in Westminster; with himself at the head of the organisation, swift and complete reform was guaranteed. The bill was passed with surprisingly little opposition, probably because Peel underplayed the significance of the changes that he envisaged.

Magistrates were to have their activities confined to the judicial side, except for the chief magistrate at Bow Street who still retained his authority over the Bow Street Runners and the Horse Patrol. (These were to be kept apart from the new police.)

The Metropolitan Police Force

Colonel Charles Rowan and Richard Mayne were the first joint commissioners of the force and to them fell the task of selecting the 2,000 men that were needed. They also compiled between them the rules and regulations of the force and the job was done so well that much of the content remains to this day. One of the opening paragraphs illustrates how Peel and the commissioners viewed the role of the new police. 'It should be understood at the outset that the principal object to be obtained is the prevention of crime.'

The area covered by the Metropolitan Police Force was later to become the County of London. It was divided into seventeen districts, each with a superintendent in charge. The headquarters was to be 4, Whitehall Place, overlooking Great Scotland Yard.

To avoid a military appearance, the uniform chosen included a blue high-collared frockcoat reaching down to just above the knee with eight large brass buttons and a leather belt with a brass buckle. The trousers were blue and of durable cloth. The top hat was specially designed with a metal frame which served two purposes, that of protecting the head from injury and also serving as a stepping-stone for gaining height! Gloves and a strong baton, similar to that of the Bow Street Runners, completed the outfit.

Naturally enough, the police were unpopular at first. Partly this was due to the imposition of a Police Rate, a levy on the parish of 8d. in the pound rateable value; citizens were going to be made to pay for their increased protection. In part, too,

37 *Sir Robert Peel, 1788–1850*. No Home Secretary has rivalled the reputation of Peel. In his own day he became a household name and the police-force he set up still has 'Bobby' as one of its nicknames. The Metropolitan Police was his brain-child and most notable achievement, but his efforts in legal and prison reform were also outstanding.

38 Bow Street and the Peelers, in the late 1830s

there was still a widespread fear of any force which appeared militaristic or re-sembled the spies of the Sidmouth era. Others said that a guinea a week was too low a wage to attract men of the right calibre to serve in the force. Peel himself defended the policeman's wage as adequate:

> I have good reason for thinking that one of my police constables, if a single man, can find out of his pay of a guinea a week: 1. lodgings, 2. medical attendance, 3. very comfortable subsistence at his mess, 4. clothing; and can, after finding these save out of his pay ten shillings a week.

Although there were several open clashes with the police in the first few months of the force's existence, responsible opinion was soon coming to its defence. *The Times* in 1830 upheld the imposition of a Police Rate and scoffed at the accusations levelled at the supposed militarism of the police:

> A military force presupposes military weapons of some kind—the police have neither swords nor pistols to defend themselves; and recent cir-cumstances suffice to prove that for the preservation of their own lives, to say nothing of the public, the bits of stick with which they are at present provided are anything but an adequate protection. We ourselves have seen nothing of the police but exemplary courtesy, forbearance and propriety, great willingness to act and, when the occasion calls, to refrain from acting. Overpaid, at a guinea a week each, no rational person can consider them.

The 'Peelers' or 'Bobbies' (short for Robert) soon had their baptism of fire in London. In 1830 and 1831 ugly scenes and disturbances accompanied the pressure for Parliamentary reform. When parliament assembled the police had great difficulty in controlling the unruly crowds without calling upon the assistance of the militia. What they had to contend with, can be gauged from some of the con-fiscated handbills read out by the Home Secretary in the Commons. The following is taken from one labelled *Liberty or Death*:

Come armed. We assure you from ocular evidence that 6,000 cutlasses have been removed from the Tower for the use of Peel's bloody gang.

Other slogans said '*No Peel*' and '*Down with the Raw Lobsters*'. Despite this open truculence, the mobs were kept in check by the sole use of truncheons. There were many incidents but it was the manner in which the police prevented a repetition in London of the riots which had occurred in Bristol which really set the new police force on its feet.

By 1844 in fact the police had become such a respected and so accepted a body that *Punch* was commenting good-humouredly on a recent advertisement for tenders for the supply of the police with boots :

> Policemen's boots are of two sizes only, the too small and the too large. The latter class are by far the most numerous; so that it is easy to judge a policeman by his foot which seems about twice as big as anyone else's. These boots, or rather boats, presumably consist of leather; but they look as clumsy, awkward and inflexible, as if they were made of cast-iron. . . .

The size of policemen's feet is still very much a topic of fun but nowadays the helmet does not provoke comment such as the following—again from *Punch*:

> The hat of the policeman has been compared to a chimney-pot, where-from, however similar to it in shape and weight, it differs in the important particular of not allowing the heat and exhalations which ascend into it to escape.

J. M. Hart, *The British Police* (Allen & Unwin)
P. Pringle, *Hue and Cry* (Museum Press 1955)

Further Reading

6 Prisons and Hangings

In November 1965, there were 817 women and 28,667 men detained in prison and Borstal institutions in this country. The number seems large, and prison reformers today cry out against the poor and overcrowded conditions in which many criminals live. But while arguments rage as to the nature and efficacy of certain types of punishment, the prisoner today might at least take some comfort from the fact that in past centuries conditions have been much worse.

Prior to the Elizabethan period there were few prisons, the principal places of detention being the common gaols. Of these there were perhaps two hundred, operated by diverse town or country authorities. They were mainly places in which men awaited the opening of the courts and were often referred to as the antechamber to the gallows. By the end of the sixteenth century imprisonment as a form of punishment became more widely used, especially for debtors and vagrants. The gaoler ran his place for profit, usually, and made his livelihood exacting fees for all services and food beyond the 'county bread' which he was required by an Elizabethan statute to give to convicted felons. Conditions in local prisons and also in the large London prisons were barbarous beyond description. Suffering, starvation, disease and filth were the lot of any prisoner who could not afford to pay for better things. The following extract from Stubbes' *Anatomie of Abuses* (1585) is not in any way an exaggeration:

> Beleve me, it greeveth me to heare (walking in the streetes) the pittifull and miserable complayntes of poore prisoners in durance for debte, and like so to continue all their life, destitute of libertie, meate, drink (though of the meanest sorte), and clothing to their backes, lying in filthie straw and lothsome dung, worse than anie dogge, voyde of all charitable consolation and brotherly comforte in this worlde, wishing and thirsting after deathe to set them at libertie and loose them from their shackles . . . and iron bandes.

Not all the convicted men stayed in prison. Many escaped their loathsome environment only to grace the scaffold and provide entertainment for the hordes of people who regularly turned up to see the mass executions. To be present at a public hanging or burning was considered by many to be a good holiday. This attitude prevailed until well into the nineteenth century. Thomas Platter in his *Travels in England* (1599) describes the regular occurrence of mass executions in London:

> There is a slaughtering and a hanging, and from all the prisons (of which there are several scattered about the town where they ask alms of the passers by, and sometimes they collect so much by their begging that they can purchase their freedom) people are taken and tried,—when the trial is over, those condemned to the rope are placed on a cart, each one with a rope about his neck, and the hangman drives with them out of the town to the gallows, called Tyburn, almost an hour away from the city,

there he fastens them up one after another by the rope and drives the cart off under the gallows which is not very high off the ground—then the criminals' friends come and draw them down by their feet, that they may die all the sooner. They are then taken down from the gallows and buried in the neighbouring cemetery.

In the seventeenth century Samuel Pepys records in his diary how he witnessed a public execution. He paid one shilling to stand on a cartwheel for an hour before-hand and reckoned that between twelve and fourteen thousand people were thronging the streets.

Just as the machinery for policing and the maintenance of law and order changed little from Elizabethan times up to the Victorian age, so did the state of the prisons. Rather the conditions in many prisons became worse. Not until the 1835 Prisons Act were inspectors appointed to visit prisons and make reports on them to the Home Office. Before this there were few regular, official visitations. Many magistrates refused to visit the gaols to which they sent convicted men for fear of catching 'gaol fever'. The conditions in Newgate were so bad that gaol fever was carried by prisoners to the court and the lord mayor, two judges, several jurymen and counsel

39 Transport ship. Most magistrates thought transportation was more humane and incidentally less expensive than imprisonment in England. On board, however, the convicts were often treated worse than the negro slaves. Many died en route, punishment was brutal and no provision was made for a return passage on completion of a sentence.

died. This prompted the authorities into action—the prison was cleaned! Few people thought in terms of the rehabilitation of prisoners after a period of enforced separation from the rest of society. Indeed, the prevailing attitude (still held by many people today) was that crime could only be kept to reasonable proportions by making the stay of the criminal in prison as unpleasant as possible. This fell into line with the 'deterrent' effect of savage punishments, and as the authorities found crimes on the increase throughout the eighteenth century, so the penalties became more severe.

Conditions in prisons also grew worse. The system whereby the gaoler extorted fees continued. In 1728 Thomas Bambridge bought the office of Warden of Fleet Prison from John Huggins for £5,000 and, in his attempts to make it show a profit, caused a scandal and a parliamentary inquiry. Subsequent on this all the debtors in Fleet Prison and elsewhere were released—97,248 of them, according to one contemporary. This type of governmental action was quite exceptional. In general, central government was unwilling to finance and take over control of what was considered the concern of the locality, the borough or county. And while this attitude was held, it was unlikely that there would be much change.

Prison Reformers

Not many influential voices were raised for the reform of the prisons until the latter part of the eighteenth century. By then the rapid growth of population and expansion of the towns and cities had caused the poor state of the prisons to deteriorate further. Much of this was naturally due to over-crowding. Prison reformers, like Oglethorpe and John Howard in the late eighteenth century, and Sir Samuel Romilly, Wilberforce and Elizabeth Fry in the early nineteenth century, regularly visited and reported upon the shocking state of the prisons. They found totally inadequate buildings and the barbaric treatment of prisoners, many of whom were flogged or punished by solitary confinement in dark, damp underground cells. They describe the transportation of prisoners to Australia as carelessly organised and inhuman; judges like Braxfield in Scotland could send numerous offenders off to Australia in the 1790s in cheerful ignorance—it came out later that he did not really know what transportation meant!

John Howard (1726–90)

From the time he was appointed Sheriff of Bedfordshire in 1773, he used his official position to remedy and publicise the shocking conditions prevailing in the prisons. In 1777 his book *State of Prisons* laid bare his discoveries of abuse and squalor. He campaigned for acts authorising local authorities to build and control local prisons. Conditions were made worse at this time since transportation, the major penalty short of execution had come to an end with the loss of the American Colonies, and was replaced by sentences of imprisonment. Only the shipping of convicts into old hulks which lay on the Thames and other rivers relieved the critical situation—Thousands lived in utmost misery in these hulks until the discovery of Australia made possible the resumption of transportation in 1787 first to New South Wales and later to Van Dieman's Land (Tasmania). Even so the hulks were not finally abandoned until 1858. Howards efforts were rewarded in 1791 with the first general Prison's Act of 1791. This provided for the establishment of

40 *The Chain Gang, on Van Dieman's Island, 1831*. In 1788 Captain Arthur Phillip landed at Botany Bay with 200 marines guarding 700 convicts. Until 1830 convicts outnumbered free immigrants in Australia. Not until sheep rearing and the discovery of gold gave prospects of wealth, did more settlers arrive. The desire to avoid the convicts of New South Wales and Van Dieman's Island helped settle Victoria in 1817. When transportation to Van Dieman's Island ceased in 1853 the island was renamed Tasmania in an effort to wipe out past memories.

national prisons on a cellular system (divided into small cells), but unfortunately this was not made obligatory and, as no provision was made for the inspection and supervision of prisons, the old practices continued in most districts.

Elizabeth Fry (1780–1845)

Elizabeth Fry, the Quaker, is famous for her campaign in the early nineteenth century for the improvement of the conditions in prisons. She was particularly concerned with the fate of female prisoners. A self-appointed reformer and prison inspector, she commanded wide respect in the early stages of her campaign. In 1813 she first visited Newgate Prison and was horrified by what she saw. From 1817 onwards she steadfastly worked for such improvements as a standard humane type of discipline; the separation of criminals—not only men from women offenders—but also hardened vicious criminals from first offenders, etc; better conditions for people being transported; rehabilitation—preparing the criminal for a useful part in society at the end of his sentence; the abolition of cruel punishments and the death penalty.

Even today her views, in the light of the recent abolition of the death penalty, command respect; the issues involved are very much alive. The recent post-war upsurge in serious and violent crime, juvenile delinquency and vandalism has given rise to substantial support in some sections of the community for the advocates of the 'cat' (flogging with a nine-stranded whip) and hanging.

When Elizabeth Fry and her brother made a tour of Northern prisons in 1818, they visited Wakefield Prison which was representative of the many prisons in the new industrial districts of Yorkshire and Lancashire. It was a prison which had been built for 110 people but which normally housed 300. In 1810 406 men and 93 women had been confined there together and by 1817 as many as 1,602 men and 278 women were crushed in.

This remarkable increase in the number of prisoners illustrates both the disorder

65

of the period and the repressive attitude taken by the authorities. Wakefield was in the heart of the factory areas.

Not all the prisons visited were as bad. In some, the prisoners were encouraged to work and pay for their keep by the products of their labour—at the Preston house of correction, when visited by Elizabeth and John Gurney, there were 150 men and 80 women, and hardly one of them was idle. The aged, the nursing mother and vagrants picked and cleaned cotton. Long servers were taught to weave and prisoners generally worked six hours in winter and ten in summer. But in others, such as Newgate, conditions made for a criminals' playground. Fighting, drinking and animal-like behaviour were tolerated by the authorities. Food was scarce and of poor quality, bedding and soap were practically non-existent and no attempt was made to introduce either discipline or a system of work. More punitive institutions would have women and children treading a wheel for up to twelve hours per day. In the Berwick Borough Gaol, prisoners were confined to their sleeping cells almost entirely and those guilty of more serious crimes were chained to the wall to keep them from causing trouble.

Other reformers testify to the terrible state of prisons in the nineteenth century. Thomas Fowell Buxton, Elizabeth Fry's brother-in-law, was especially interested

41 *Prison ship,* in Portsmouth Harbour, 1828. When the prisons were filled to overflowing many old ships were taken over. The 'hulks' or prison ships lying in the Thames were the centres of indescribable squalor and disease. Many convicts awaiting transportation never managed to leave the country.

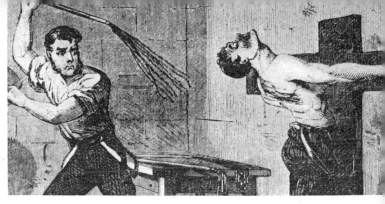

42 Flogging at Newgate. The 'Cat o' Nine tails' was used indiscriminately in many prisons in the early nineteenth century, though in some a more humane approach was attempted.

in the causes of juvenile crime and he produced in 1818 *An Enquiry whether Crime and Misery are produced or prevented by our present system of Prison Discipline.* He questioned the existing arrangements because first-time offenders and even innocent people were likely to be corrupted by others. An impassioned plea for reform was made when he wrote of the probable fate of men who had been arrested and were still untried. They were punished almost as soon as they were taken into custody:

> The prisoner, after his commitment is made out, is handcuffed to a file of perhaps a dozen wretched persons in a similar situation, and marched through the streets, sometimes a considerable distance, followed by a crowd of impudent and insulting boys—exposed to the gaze and stare of every passenger. The moment he enters the prison, irons are hammered onto him; then he is cast into a compound of all that is disgusting and depraved. At night he is locked up in a narrow cell, with perhaps half-a-dozen of the worst thieves in London, or as many vagrants, whose rags are alive and in actual motion with vermin; he may find himself in bed and in bodily contact between a robber and a murderer.... He is habituated to idleness and reconciled with filth and familiarised with crime.... Receiving him because he is too bad for society, you return him to the world, impaired in health, debased in intellect and corrupted in principles.

Written pleas for the reform of prisons such as this by Buxton did not go unnoticed. At this time a parliamentary committee was looking into the question of penal reform and Elizabeth Fry was called before it to give her views. She outlined to the committee her picture of an ideal gaol for women, in which she maintained that solitary confinement should be reserved for the most vicious of women prisoners.

Some of her views, and those of many other reformers on the separation of criminals into different categories so that the less-hardened and more reformable might not be contaminated, were incorporated into the new prisons built towards the middle of the century. The complete separation of prisoners typified by the American State Penitentiary at Philadelphia was slow to find favour in England, but the Pentonville new model prison of the 1840s isolated inmates at first and then, after a time, they were allowed to associate with others—in silence! Elizabeth's comment, on seeing the partly-built prison at Pentonville in 1841, was: 'I think that a prison for separate confinement should be so constructed that the culprits may at least see the sky.'

She was ahead of her time in her views on the punishment of prisoners. Strict prison discipline was sufficient punishment in itself, she thought, and if discipline was accompanied by Christian kindness, crime would be diminished because many criminals were capable of reform. The prison authorities did not, in general, take kindly to Elizabeth's criticisms. Her visitations and Bible-readings to the prisoners were regarded as the actions of an idealist who was unaware of the criminal mind. No doubt, many of the inmates of the prisons remained unreformed, but at least much of their environment was changed for the better, if only because of the publicity which attended gaol-visiting. Her battle to soften up the punishments inflicted also caused unpopularity. She objected to such practices as putting women on a treadwheel for hours at a stretch each day. 'The female character is rarely improved by such rough and laborious occupation.' In its place she advocated cooking, needlework and knitting so that they were more prepared to play their proper part in society when they came out.

Flogging was regarded as a brutal and useless punishment. 'We are of the opinion that flogging is so injurious in its tendency that it much tends to harden to make them more degenerate, and what is very injurious, it does not appear to deter from crime, for after a prisoner has had a very severe flogging he began again in a day or two, especially the Boys.'

Most of the men sentenced to death at this time were reprieved, often at the last moment, for the conviction that terror ought to deter men from crime was balanced by the recognition that wholesale slaughter was out of the question. Elizabeth stoutly maintained that the deterrent theme was useless and that the hardened criminal was quite unmoved by it. She told the authorities that criminals shared 'the predestinarian notion vulgarly prevalent among thieves—that if they are to be hanged, they are to be hanged, and nothing can prevent it'. Probably her campaign in this sphere, when allied to the efforts of reformers like Romilly and Mackintosh, helped the passage of the Act of 1837 which reduced the number of capital offences from thirty-seven to sixteen.

43 Elizabeth Fry reading to prisoners in Newgate, 1823. Her bible readings played a major role in her attempt to promote the spiritual and material welfare of those who would soon face death or removal overseas.

44 Dr Palmer the notorious poisoner at his execution in 1856.

Transportation

The simple quick solution to the problem of prison overcrowding and the easiest way to wash one's hands of criminals was to ship them off to the colonies. Since the seventeenth century transportation had acted as a kind of safety valve for the turbulent and criminal in society. After the loss in 1783 of the traditional dumping ground, the American colonies, Captain Cook's discovery of Australia provided another outlet. Between 1788 and 1868, 160,663 (including 23,500 women) were shipped there. In the 1820s an average of five ships a year were sent. Many magistrates thought that transportation was good for all concerned; for the mother country disposed of its troublemakers, the country receiving the convicts was colonised, and the criminal benefited since he was thought to have a good chance of making a new life. Some there were who objected to transportation because they thought that crimes were sometimes deliberately committed so as to gain free passage to better opportunities. Perhaps they were right. When, in 1836, prison inspectors visited Liverpool, transportation overseas was urged because they found the environment so bad for juveniles. In an overcrowded port, full of immigrants and drifters, few juveniles received any education other than that afforded by the streets. Almost anywhere else would have been far more suitable for them.

The system of transportation in some ways delayed reform of prison conditions. It was an alternative to the death penalty for many serious crimes and it meant that English prisons were crowded with short-sentence people, often the minor offenders such as the drunkards, street-fighters and poachers. From 1830 onwards, however, opposition to convict-dumping grew stronger from the Australians. As soon as any formal, thriving society appeared the convicts were as unwanted there as in England. In 1868 transportation was finally abolished.

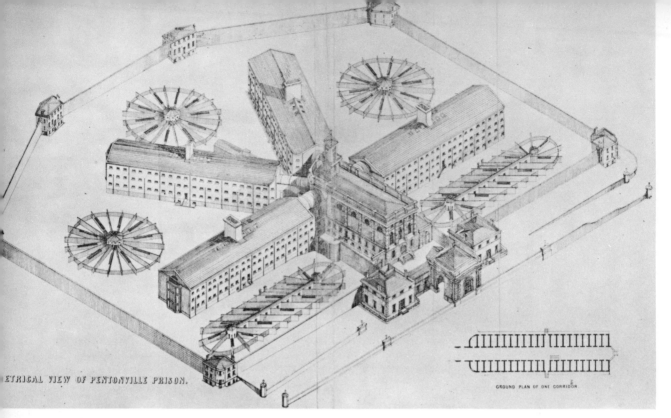

ETRICAL VIEW OF PENTONVILLE PRISON.

GROUND PLAN OF ONE CORRIDOR.

45 Pentonville Prison in 1845. Solitary confinement was considered to have a positive value and reformers such as John Howard had urged its merits, at least during the night. The system, pioneered at Philadelphia by a Quaker governor, aimed to produce 'that calm contemplation which brings repentance'—and all English prisons built after Pentonville in 1842 employed the cell system. Notice the individual exercise yards. After a long period of solitary confinement prisoners were allowed to associate for employment on public works. The workshops and other facilities came much later. Solitary confinement disappeared in the 1920s and is now only used on rare occasions for offences against prison discipline.

The overall picture of prison conditions in the early decades of the nineteenth century was one of either barbaric treatment or overindulgence. The trouble really stemmed from the fact that there was no real system. Prisons were largely independent and run on the local money of the borough or county; there was no central national body to organise reform or insist on regular standards. This was to come later in 1888. The campaigns of groups of people like the Gurneys exposed many shortcomings and prodded the authorities into some reforms. Elizabeth Fry's initial success at Newgate, her introduction of orderly discipline, teaching, Bible classes and readings, effected some improvements but to a large extent they were short-lived. One of the biggest obstacles was the persistent problem of numbers and the reluctance of the authorities to spend large sums of public money on the swift erection of new buildings. This problem is still with us today.

Just how influential and effective Elizabeth Fry's campaigns proved is hard to ascertain. She gave evidence to a Parliamentary Committee set up in 1831 to review punishments for statistics had shown a considerable increase in crime despite the introduction of Peel's police in 1829. Elizabeth maintained that, perhaps because the prisons were improving and because prosecutions were cheaper, magistrates were more inclined to send criminals to prison. The official attitude is clear from the reply they gave her:

> Does not the whole of your view tend rather to the encouragement of crime in the present state of society than to its prevention? Or, at all events, does it sufficiently effect the great work of prevention?

In 1861 the list of capital offences was reduced to four; murder, treason, piracy and destruction of arsenals and shipyards. At the same time transportation came to an end and these two factors meant a change in the attitude to imprisonment. Obviously if most criminals at some stage were to be released to live amongst their fellow men, then more emphasis would be required on the reformative aspects of the penal system, but this change was a long time in coming. *Improvements to the Penal System*

Soon after Pentonville opened in 1842, fifty-two new prisons were built on the same plan, providing altogether 11,000 separate cells, and apart from the new open prisons of recent years most of the prisons today date back to this period. The system, however, was expressly punitive; the idea being that inmates should experience solitary and dreary labour. In 1846 the 'crank' was introduced, to provide a prisoner with occupation in his cell. He had to turn a heavy crank a certain number of times each day, entirely unproductively. There were certain places, like Birmingham and Wakefield, which experimented in employing prisoners in useful labour, but they were in a minority. Little was done to improve prison diet; the

46 Female Convicts at work during the silent hour in Brixton Prison.

47 *Civil prisoners.* Most people think that debtors' prisons were abolished in Dickens' times. Imprisonment for debt still exists and over ten per cent of the prison population consists of men who are committed for contempt of court over non-payment of wife-maintenance, income tax, etc.

introduction of potatoes was frowned upon, lest the prisoners should eat better 'than many of the humbler classes'. Even when the prisons act of 1877 authorised the state, through the Home Office, to take over all the prisons (it was the first social service to be nationalised), the punitive philosophy was still in existence. Hard labour, hard fare and hard beds were the order of the day. A change of attitude was apparent when in 1895 a committee under the chairmanship of Herbert Gladstone condemned the punitive elements in the penal system. Acts in 1898 and 1899 abolished the crank, treadwheel, and useless hard labour. First offenders were to be treated differently and a reformatory establishment was opened in a converted prison at Borstal, Kent, for young prisoners.

In the twentieth century perhaps the most outstanding development in penal reform has been the gradual growth of constructive methods for treating law-breakers. The 1908 Probation of Offenders Act and the subsequent acts of 1914 and 1925 made possible a comprehensive and efficient probation service for both adults and juveniles. The pattern for the future was inaugurated in 1923 with the Wakefield prison experiments—prisoners were allowed to eat in associated groups and educational and recreational activities were organised for them. By 1936 the Wakefield system included a camp where prisoners under minimum security were employed fully on farming activities, and were even paid for their work. By this time the Borstal system had been greatly extended and included separate establishments for girls. A landmark in attempts at constructive treatment came in 1948 with the Criminal Justice Act. This abolished the old prison classifications and penal servitude—imprisonment covered all normal committals. The act embodied clauses which attempted treatment appropriate to the needs and abilities of the prisoners. Three new forms of treatment were introduced:

1. Detention centres for up to six months for the young offenders aged between fourteen and seventeen and seventeen and twenty-one.

2. Corrective training for between two and four years for recidivists (people who returned to prison) over the age of twenty-one.

3. Prolonged preventive detention lasting for up to fourteen years for persistent offenders over thirty.

Elizabeth Fry and other early nineteenth century prison reformers might have been proud of the progress so far made, but even so the Howard League for penal reform and other reforming bodies (and indeed society at large) can still find much room for improvement.

J. Howard, *State of Prisons* ed. K. Ruck (Everyman 1929)
Winifred A. Elkin, *English Penal System* (Pelican 1957)
W. Andrews, *Bygone Punishments* (1931)
John Kent, *Elizabeth Fry* (Batsford 1962)

Further Reading

7 Victorian Era—Apple-pie Order

The close of the Napoleonic Wars in 1815 inaugurated a period of unprecedented peace and the industrialisation of Britain continued in full swing. The population was more than doubled in the reign of Queen Victoria (1837–1901); even so, the majority enjoyed a better standard of living than had ever been known before. Karl Marx, writing in the 1840s, had forecast a violent revolution engineered by the working classes, for he had witnessed personally many of the worst aspects of the early stages of the industrial revolution. He would have been amazed to find that by the end of the century the working classes were putting their faith and energies into peaceful reform through parliamentary action, rather than by the violent overthrow of existing 'capitalist' institutions. This was because, at the same time as Britain was undergoing a prolonged industrial revolution, moderate and gradual political reforms were brought about. The growing wealth of the country and the extension of the franchise by the Reform Bills of 1832, 1867 and 1884 helped gain for Britain the envy of much of the world; she was renowned for her constitution and the production of manufactured goods. Napoleon had described the British derogatively as a nation of shop-keepers; by the mid-nineteenth century Britain was known as the workshop of the world.

The process of industrialisation and urbanisation described in Chapter 3 was accelerated in the first decades of the nineteenth century. And, as the basic structure of society changed, so did the ideas of how the country should be governed.

We have seen already how the policing arrangements and means of ensuring law and order had proved totally inadequate for an expanding, urban and industrialised society. The first tentative and money-pinching efforts to tackle the problem have also been described. This, however, is only one aspect of the vast change that came about in the Victorian age. In setting up a Metropolitan Police Force and reforming the penal code, Peel had carefully put into operation some of the measures for which perceptive reformers had long agitated. Others, who were appalled at the inadequacy of the machinery of government and administration bequeathed to them by the eighteenth century, were just as careful and systematic. They set out to discuss people's needs and, when they found that all was far from well, facts were accumulated and arguments assembled to facilitate reform. John Howard, Sir Samuel Romilly, Elizabeth Fry and others had pioneered reform in the penal system. Their method of publicising the facts they discovered was soon emulated by Parliament. Parliamentary Committees, Parliamentary Commissions, Select Committees, returns and statistical tables became a part of the law-making process. Government gradually became less a matter of playing by ear as it had been in the eighteenth century and more the practice of reading the music in front of one. The ideas of Jeremy Bentham (1748–1832) became widespread. He advocated greater efficiency in the administrative machinery of the state; if institutions were demonstratably inefficient then they should be scrapped or overhauled. The principle that he and his followers (called the 'Utilitarians') followed was that of usefulness. The state should be so organised that the greatest happiness of the greatest number was sought after. This principle caused the state to extend its powers so that for the public good private rights were often invaded. For example, the Public Health Acts, after cholera scares, enforced proper drainage and safer sanitation upon various local authorities. The same principle can be observed in the compulsory setting up of police forces in the provinces in 1856 and later in the acts concerning compulsory education. Some of the reforms and advances of the early Victorian era can be ascribed to the awakening of a social conscience. Whereas Wilberforce and others had struggled to abolish slavery and achieved their end after almost forty years, by the 1830s many people in authority were beginning to seek out evils, so that they could put them right.

By mid-Victorian times it seemed that society was well on the way to solving most of the problems which its introspection had unearthed. In 1851 the Great Exhibition in the Crystal Palace had put on display to the rest of the world Britain's great lead in science and the manufacturing of goods and at that time her position was unchallenged. Railways had been laid all over Britain and were visible proof of her expansion of industry, her skill and inventiveness. The extension of her internal communications caused the country to be more closely knit and unified and hastened the expansion of cities and specialisation of industries.

The self-confidence exemplified by the Great Exhibition is reflected in the philosophy of the mid-Victorians. The middle classes, proud of their industry, thrift and sobriety, extolled these virtues. To them the eighteenth century seemed associated with dissoluteness, and with bribery and corruption in politics. The growing prosperity of the country, the influence of Wesleyanism on the moral regeneration of society, the extension of the franchise and the introduction of vote by ballot in 1867, putting an end to corruption at parliamentary elections—all these factors caused rectitude to become the accepted norm rather than the exception. So, too, the respect for authority which is so much a Victorian trait, helped cause greater stability and order in society. For most of the nineteenth century it was generally thought that there were those whose place it was to give orders and others whose duty it was to carry them out. Obedience was a virtue highly-prized; even a woman's place in the home reflected this attitude. (However, the chivalrous attitude adopted towards the 'weaker' sex helped somewhat the move towards more civilised and humane behaviour.)

If the mid-Victorian attitude was one of confidence, then this might easily be ascribed to the fact that England had escaped the bloodshed and revolutions which had been part and parcel of the history of the continental countries in the fifty-odd years which followed the French Revolution. Up to 1850 many people of property had feared that the same might happen in England. After 1850 this prospect faded.

During the first half of the century outbreaks such as the Luddite rioting, the social distress after Waterloo, the troubled twenties, the violence preceding the first Reform Bill of 1832 and the great working-class agitations associated with the Chartist Movement, had all caused the authorities a great deal of anxiety.

75

Chartism   This movement was one of the most dynamic of working-class associations. It was also the one most feared by the authorities in the late thirties and forties. The people who made up this radical movement were partly those who had been disappointed with the moderation of the Reform Bill of 1832, and also those who had seen Robert Owen's experiments in trade unionism fail in 1834. Well-to-do London artisans joined forces with disillusioned trade unionists and with the discontented masses in the industrial North. The leaders, William Lovett and Francis Place, drew up in 1838 the 'People's Charter'. It called for six demands: universal male suffrage, annual parliaments, equal electoral districts, the removal of the property qualification for membership of Parliament, the payment of members, and a secret ballot. It is difficult for us to appreciate how radical these demands were at that time. All except the call for annual parliaments have become part of our present-day parliamentary system.

To the middle and upper classes who were represented in the Commons, these demands appeared tantamount to revolution. This danger became more apparent when the Chartist riots accompanied the three petitions which were made to Parliament, each launched at a time of great economic distress—1839, 1842 and 1848. The petitions were preceded by big public meetings, intensive and fiery propaganda and general popular agitation. From the centres of London, Birmingham and Leeds 'The Charter' became the battle-cry of a nation-wide movement. In the spring of 1839 the National Convention met in London and then withdrew to Birmingham. There was general excitement and a hint of civil war in the air. Count Chopski, a Polish exile, published articles on revolutionary tactics and pamphlets were sold on how to build barricades. When Parliament rejected the monster petition for which hundreds and thousands of signatures had been collected, there was a danger of large-scale fighting breaking out. The resulting conflicts were a disappointment to those advocates of physical force such as Feargus O'Connor, the hot-headed Irish radical. Despite local strikes and petty insurrections, a wild riot in Birmingham was put down, and an attack in Newport was concluded outside the Queen's Hotel where a dozen men were killed by the military. From then onwards Chartism was effectively dead. The southern moderates under Lovett sought their aims by peaceful agitation and the extension of popular education, whilst the violent elements under O'Connor became more extreme and isolated. After another abortive petition and demonstration in 1842, with its attendant riots and strikes, more leaders were imprisoned or transported. Nevertheless, the authorities in London still took elaborate precautions against the movement during the presentation of the third petition in 1848. The Peelers were out in force, 170,000 special constables were sworn in and put on duty, and businessmen barricaded their windows and made ready their pistols. A showdown with the lower-class radicals was anticipated, even looked forward to with relish by many. In the end, O'Connor's followers were prevailed upon to disperse and the petition, weighing over five hundredweight was taken to Westminster in three cabs; when it was discovered that it contained many bogus signatures, such as Sir Robert Peel, 'Mr. Punch' and 'Victoria Rex', the last demonstration by the Chartists was virtually laughed off the stage.

48 *Chartist Riots at Newport, 1839.* John Frost, a draper and former mayor of Newport, led 4,000 men to release Henry Vincent, a Chartist Leader, from gaol. The authorities were ready and soldiers barricaded in a hotel killed several of the rioting out-of-work miners. Frost and others were arrested and were transported after their death sentence was commuted. The Newport riots heralded the decline of Chartism as many of its middle-class supporters shied away from violent methods.

Here is one interpretation of the events and an eyewitness account of the 1848 demonstration by Charles Greville. It goes a long way towards explaining the mid-Victorian confidence in their ability to put things right; it also illustrates the feeling that lawlessness and disorder were soon to become a thing of the past:

> Monday passed off with surprising quiet, and it was considered a most satisfactory demonstration on the part of the Government, and the peaceable and loyal part of the community. Enormous preparations were made, and a host of military, police, and special constables were ready if wanted; every gentleman in London was sworn, and during a great part of the day, while the police were reposing, they did duty. The Chartist movement was contemptible; but everybody rejoices that the defensive demonstration was made, for it has given a great and memorable lesson; and it will produce a vast effect in all foreign countries, and show how solid is the foundation on which we are resting. We have displayed a great resolution and a great strength, and given unmistakeable proofs, that if sedition and rebellion hold up their heads in this country, they will be instantly met with the most vigorous resistance, and be put down by the hand of authority, and by the zealous co-operation of all classes of the people. . . .
>
> . . . In the morning (a very fine day) everybody was on the alert; the parks were closed; our office was fortified, a barricade of Council Registers was erected in the accessible room on the ground-floor, and all our guns were taken down to be used in defence of the building. However, at about twelve o'clock crowds came streaming along Whitehall, going northwards, and it was announced that all was over. The intended

77

tragedy was rapidly changed into a ludicrous farce. The Chartists, about 20,000 in number, assembled on Kennington Common. Presently Mr. Mayne appeared on the ground, and sent one of his inspectors to say he wanted to speak to Feargus O'Connor to inform him that the meeting would not be interfered with, but the procession would not be allowed. Feargus insisted on shaking hands with Mayne, swore he was his best of friends, and instantly harangued his rabble, advising them not to provoke a collision, and to go away quietly—advice they instantly obeyed, and with great alacrity and good humour. Thus all evaporated in smoke. The petition was brought down piecemeal and presented in the afternoon. Since that there has been an exposure of the petition itself, covering the authors of it with ridicule and disgrace. It turns out to be signed by less than two millions, instead of by six as Feargus stated; and of those, there were no end of fictitious names, together with the insertion of every species of ribaldry, indecency, and impertinence.

CHARLES CAVENDISH FULKE GREVILLE

The Greville Memoirs: Second Part (1885)

After the Chartist movement collapsed any real danger of revolution and wholesale disorder in society disappeared. Better living standards for most, the channeling of working-class reforming activity into trade unionism and later into the Labour Party, at the end of the century; the spread of state education after the Education Act of 1870; the growth in efficiency and numbers of the police; the increased sense of responsibility which the extension of the franchise caused; the emergence by the end of the century of the first signs of the Welfare State; all these factors helped promote better law and order in English society.

Violence, though, was still present beneath the surface of Victorian calm; it only became apparent in times of distress and these were mercifully infrequent.

The Extension of the Police System

By 1840, 108 boroughs had established their own police force. It was compulsory for the counties in 1856. In London, Peel's original force of 2,000 men soon expanded and reached 5,500 by 1850, covering a police district which had increased sixfold. However, there was no separate detective force until a particularly brutal murder in 1842 by Daniel Good in Roehampton caused widespread public alarm. A force of two Inspectors and six Sergeants was then set up to deal with exceptional crimes. A contemporary journal told its readers that, to investigate such practices as forgery and confidence-tricks, 'a superior order of Police is requisite, whose duty it is to wear no uniform and to perform the most difficult operations of their craft. . . . Sometime they are called upon to investigate robberies so executed that no human ingenuity appears to ordinary observers capable of finding the thief. He leaves no trail or trace. Every clue seems cut off; but the experience of a detective guides him into tracks quite invisible to other eyes.' We are fast moving into the world of Sir Arthur Conan Doyle and Sherlock Holmes! *Punch* in an article in 1845 was not so complimentary about the three-years-old detective branch:

'Its members, disguised in plain clothes, are now known to mix in all societies, to whose manners and peculiarities they are instructed to adapt themselves. They mingle, as exquisites, in the 'salons' of fashion; they

49 (left) *A Peeler of 1837–38,* from a drawing by Lucien Besche.

50 Tom Smith—a well-known London policeman in the fifties and sixties. The top-hat was worn as late as 1860.

creep, as cads, into the 'crib' of the costermonger. They frequent every species of tavern, from the first-rate to the Jerry-shop; and neither the freedom of the tap nor the sanctity of the parlour is safe from their intrusion. . . . But the evil does not stop here. In his uniform the Policeman is notorious for scraping acquaintance with servants at area-railings. . . . How much longer are free-born Englishmen to submit to the espionage, and to be victimised by the voracity of an X10, a Y15 or a Z20?"

The police, since their inception, have always borne the brunt of public criticism when disorder occurs. The sixties proved a troublesome time for them. They had difficulty in apprehending the perpetrators of violent forms of crime which broke out in 1862—'garotting', or throttling and stunning from behind. Even a Member of Parliament was robbed in this way. In 1866 they had to cope with the massed demonstration organised by the Reform League. Police Notices banned a meeting in Hyde Park and, although 3,000 police were on duty, the ensuing disorder could only be put down with the assistance of the Life Guards. Further evidence of their unpopularity at this time can be gleaned from the illustrations in *Punch* which showed the effects of the recently granted permission for the police to wear beards and moustaches. It seemed that the police were showing—according to a November issue of the *Daily Telegraph* in 1868—a 'delicate forebearance' to the criminals of the day. *Punch* commented adversely on Richard Mayne's order to his constables to confiscate children's hoops. These were made of cast iron and supposedly a danger and a nuisance to the public. Judy dedicated this ditty to the

Commissioner:

> The hoop-stealers of London,
> Who call themselves police,
> But leave the classes criminal
> Most carefully in peace.
>
> The hoop-stealers of London
> Who never, never shrink
> From taking bribes to see or not,
> And ne'er refuse a drink.

Punch maintained that they had more important work to do than to take away children's playthings—and *Punch* was right. They were busy during the Fenian outrages—Irish-American conspirators who, in 1867 and 1883, campaigned for Home Rule for Ireland—and police were constantly on guard against bomb threats. They safeguarded important buildings such as the Houses of Parliament and the Law Courts. In the 1890s they coped competently with the bomb threats of the Anarchist society—in fact the Special Branch of detectives was formed specifically to deal with such dangerous movements. The period leading up to the First World War was a testing time for the police. Violence, engendered by trade union activities, strikes, lock-outs, the Irish troubles and the suffragette movement, kept the police on their toes. In 1911, during the Siege of Sidney Street, they had the Home Secretary in person, Winston Churchill, following the battle being

51 *The Police wear beards*

52 'Specials' being instructed, 1887. A trade depression in the 1870s and 80s caused massive unemployment. The emerging socialist party organised open-air meetings for unskilled workers. On 13 November 1887, 'Bloody Sunday', a pitched battle took place between police and workers in which two people were killed and over 100 injured. Order was restored by the Life Guards. (The biggest strike came two years later in 1889 when the London dockers went on strike for a 'tanner an hour'.)

waged against a gang which was armed with fourteen automatic weapons. The years 1910–12 were full of industrial distress and rioting, and troops on more than one occasion were called upon to fire.

The late eighties and the nineties had been a period of great strikes in industry, ranging from the famous 'Dockers' Tanner strike of 1889 to the engineers' strike of 1897. Though the new Labour Party, founded at the turn of the century, succeeded in guiding much of the trade union militancy into constitutional and parliamentary channels, the rapid growth of the trade unions caused much industrial unrest and violence. In the same period, Mrs Pankhurst formed the Women's Social and Political Union in Manchester. This suffragette movement publicised their grievances by chaining their members to railings, breaking windows and interrupting political meetings. After 1912 the extremists caused havoc by throwing bombs, cutting telephone wires, burning buildings and similar crimes. When arrested, the women went on hunger strike in prison, and had to be forcibly fed and even released because of their desire for martyrdom. In 1913 Miss Emily Davison went to the lengths of flinging herself under the hooves of the King's horse in the Derby, so strong were her convictions. Such open resort to violence brought

81

53 The Sidney Street Siege, 1911: Winston Churchill (then Home Secretary), looking on during the siege of the Anarchists.

54 Suffragettes being taken into custody. After the strikes and industrial unrest of 1910–12 the police had the awkward task of dealing with female fanatics agitating for the vote. Houses, schools and a railway station were set on fire and a bomb was found beneath the Coronation Chair in Westminster Abbey. They received the vote in the Fifth Parliamentary Reform Bill of 1928.

to a close the extraordinary peace and self-confidence of the Victorian age. A different philosophy, a changed Britain emerged from the blood-bath of the Great War.

One of the best examples of the peaceful use of the police came during the General Strike of 1926. In May, the Washington correspondent in London wrote home, 'I have seen more fighting in one night of a local steel strike in Pittsburg than there has been in all England this week.' Much of this lack of violence can be attributed directly to the tactful handling of the crowds by the police. This indeed has tended to become one of the hallmarks of a good police force. During the fascist demonstrations and display of physical force in the thirties, through to the handling of Guy Fawkes' Day celebrations and the anti-nuclear force demonstrations of the present day, the British police have shown remarkable restraint and tact in their handling of crowds. The lesson of Peterloo has been well-learned.

Further Reading

F. C. Mather, *Public Order in the Age of the Chartists* (Manchester University Press 1959)
Peter Quennell (ed.), *Mayhew's Londons* (1944)
  London's Underworld (1950)

8 The Present and the Future?

We have so far traced the history of law and order in England. Civil law, that which deals with disputes in court between individuals, has been largely omitted. So too has the growing complexity of the legal system as society has become more civilised and sophisticated. (Details of the present-day legal system and the cases that different courts try can be found in the books listed at the end of this chapter.) The emphasis has been on the disorders of the community and how authority has dealt with them. The question inevitably arises: have we progressed, and if so, how far? Is there, in fact, in our modern state, more law and order? Are we safer in our everyday contact with fellow citizens than our ancestors have been? Do we treat the criminal element in society—which is always there—more humanely and in the best interests of our society?

Some answers can be readily given. Our behaviour is more governed by laws than ever before. The role and the responsibility of the state in the making of laws has come a long way in the last few centuries. John Locke, the great English political theorist of the seventeenth century, maintained that men were basically good but laws were still needed to keep down 'the few desperate men' in society. Law today plays a much more important and pervasive part in our lives; from birth to death we are ruled and conditioned by the rules imposed by society. The aim of the state as expressed in its criminal law is to safeguard its own existence, to maintain order and to make it possible for all of its citizens to lead a good life, free from the molestation of others. In this brief survey of law and order in England we have seen the gradual rise in the importance of the state and with it the power of law. Whereas once men thought that government was good if it was largely unnoticed or did not affect them—i.e. that good government was little government—now it plays a much more positive role. Statute law in the form of Education Acts, Noise Abatement Act, National Health and National Insurance Acts, Factory Acts, etc. aims at improving the conditions in which we live. The expansion of the scope of Criminal and Civil justice also tends to cause more of our actions to come within the compass of the law.

But there is a boundary beyond which, of necessity, the law cannot go. The penal system as it exists is a system where offences are punished because they are the one most recognisably harmful to society and also are the ones most likely to be detected and punishable. Certain moral offences are not considered to be within the sphere of law. A man may commit the seven deadly sins regularly without appearing in a courtroom, whilst other actions, such as illegal parking, which could not possibly be considered sins, could lead to state action and punishment.

On some points, though, it is difficult to give an unqualified answer. For example, almost every age has been loud in its cry that 'Crime is on the increase'. From the previous chapters it may seem apparent that crime has followed an upward spiral. Many parents today maintain that standards of public and private

55 Crowd control is an important part of the work of the police. This demonstration outside the Houses of Parliament was called by London building workers in defence of trade union rights.

behaviour are on the decline. The respect for authority that has been associated with Victorianism is also no longer apparent. This type of argument is hard to answer. For how do we measure orderliness and law in a community?

Statistics of the breaking of laws must be very carefully interpreted. Sound radio, television and the more sensational of the newspapers all tend to give prominence to the newsworthy, i.e. exceptional, behaviour of people in our society. We hear too much of the 'Mod' v. 'Rocker'-type battle on the sea front, hair-raising escapades of the 'ton-up' boys and the vandalism which expresses itself in the destructions of telephone booths or the slashing of train seats after an away soccer match. Most murder stories, too, are front-page news avidly devoured by the average peace-loving citizen.

Perhaps the best evidence that the majority of people in our society are law-abiding is this very appetite for knowledge of the anti-social behaviour of the few. Indeed, there is little doubt that, in general, people today are more civilised and have more respect for the laws which society has imposed. Many of the previous causes of riots on a large scale, and of crime, have disappeared. Few people nowadays are driven to crime by sheer necessity; the welfare state has taken care that no one need starve. As the machinery of government and the administration of laws has become more advanced so now there is more chance of receiving fair play whether as a transgressor of the laws or as a litigant before the courts. Justice, the fair execution of laws and handling of disputes is better today than ever before.

However, one would be on shaky ground if one maintained that respect for law and order and the lesser incidence of disorder is a natural consequence of our higher material civilisation. To follow this argument through, the more advanced the society, then the less crime and disorder there should be. Yet the years following the Second World War have seen a greater incidence of crime in this country—not all of it ascribable to the natural aftermath of war.

Causes of Crime   Various theories about the cause of crime have been advanced in the past. We may feel we are at last getting somewhere, if only because criminologists are beginning to say that they do not really know all that much about the causes. Obviously if one could mend the broken homes, remedy the results of neglect and poverty and stir the lazy into activity, the impossible would be near to achievement—a state in which the laws were universally kept and respected.

This Utopian situation is never likely to arise, but crime could be better prevented if more were known about its causes. Research units have been set up in some universities such as Cambridge and Birmingham to study past cases and analyse criminal behaviour, but this approach is still in its infancy. Certain theories advanced so far, especially by psychologists, include those of 'aggression' and 'self-assertion'—that the criminal often acts as he does because he feels deprived of either material things such as money and possessions, or lacks the love and care which most people need if they are to be 'integrated' personalities, reasonably adjusted to their everyday life. Some of these theories might fit individual cases in certain circumstances but the basic common denominator found so far is that most criminals are inadequate or immature. Only the minority are the aggressive, vicious type which naturally springs to mind when the word 'criminal' is mentioned. One governor of a prison for corrective training called the majority of his charges 'woefully insipid characters' and it is this category of person who is affected most by the breakdown of traditional close-knit units such as the family

56 Policewoman keeping contact with Headquarters. Even more up-to-date 'walkie-talkies'—transistorised pocket models—are increasingly used to fight crime and save man-power. In Lancashire a recent successful scheme was the 'neighbourhood bobby' who rarely visits headquarters but keeps close contact through his two-way radio.

and the church. No doubt the complexity of modern society and the impersonality of authority in the present-day state has much to do with it. The opportunity is there to fiddle the income-tax returns, to avoid paying train fares and such; whereas in a more localised small community fewer people cheat, if only because there is greater risk of being found out. It is in the country districts that there is not only less crime but what is committed is more readily solved. London still has the highest crime rate per head of population and the greatest number of unsolved crimes. In the counties in 1964 the proportion of crimes cleared up was 46·6 per cent, whilst that of the metropolitan area was 21·6 per cent. As the cities grow larger, is this trend going to continue?

Although difficult to interpret, the figures show signs of a remarkable increase in the past three decades. In 1965 the number of indictable offences reported to the police was 1,133,882 a rise of 6·2 per cent on 1964; more than twice the total for 1948 and almost four times that of 1938. Of these the number of murders has remained remarkably steady, averaging between 130 and 160 per annum. The number of cases of violence has risen, though, from 2,721 in 1938 to 23,470 in

Number of Crimes

87

57 *The Identikit.* The officer is building up an Identikit picture of a suspect with the help of a witness at Police Headquarters, Hutton, near Preston. This method is used increasingly, also for police requests for information on the television.

1964. In 1965 in the London area alone, the number of robbery and assault cases reached a record figure of 1,609, an increase of 27·1 per cent. The criminal taking amounted to £2,017,502, of which only £179,405 was recovered. It has been estimated by the Insurance Association that in 1964 over £34 millions were stolen.

Organised, professional crime is increasing all the time. The top criminal plans raids down to the minutest detail, employs experts and carries out one robbery to finance another. The growth of gambling clubs, drug-taking, etc. has provided them with steady incomes. The protection rackets only come into prominence when rival gangs 'carve' each other up or a hireling dies in a gun-fight. Big business crime is so well organised that even known criminals can seldom be convicted. Perhaps the recent proposal to have a majority verdict by juries instead of the traditional unanimous one will make intimidation and bribery of jurors less successful.

Besides the increased activity of the 'cosh' gangs and the professional criminals like the 'Great Train Robbers', the incidence of petty and casual crime is mounting. Stores now mobilise large forces of shop detectives to counter the growing numbers of shop-lifters. From the arrests they make it is clear that few people steal because they are kleptomaniacs or because of necessity; in most cases it is sheer greed and in the cases of juveniles, bravado. A recent case to be publicised is that of a seemingly respectable old woman who regularly hid away a tin of salmon each time she visited a self-service store, and just as surreptitiously and regularly the cost of the salmon was added to her bill!

The two biggest categories in the crime statistics—which between them add up to nine-tenths of the total—are larceny and breaking and entering. Of the one million crimes committed in 1965, more than 200,000 of them were concerned with cars. Over 100,000 vehicles were driven away without the owner's consent. Thirty-four per cent of all indictable crimes to property or money were to the value of less than £5.

The Remedies?

One way of tackling these thefts and most of the other crimes, is to reduce the opportunity and the temptation. Householders should lock their doors and windows and drivers their cars. Legislation might be introduced, as in Sweden and Germany, making anti-theft devices on cars compulsory. To combat the snatching of wages, greater use could be made of cheques. This solution would call for greater care by everyone—hardly a thing one can legislate.

The best remedy, of course, would be to ensure a far higher rate of detection, This would act as a much better deterrent than heavy punishments. At the moment in London, the chances of getting away with certain crimes are as follows: murder 10·8 per cent; burglary 71·4 per cent; robbery and assault with intent to rob 71·1 per cent. But to achieve a higher rate of success against criminal action would mean a much more drastic organisation of society, for the 'war on crime'. Some moves in this direction are already afoot. The Royal Commission recommendations of 1962 are being gradually put into effect. The Police Act has strengthened the powers of the Home Secretary; collaboration between the 152 different police forces has been improved and the police research and planning branch has shown signs of progress. To deal with the small number of intelligent and highly professional criminals, the police must be able to counter brains with brains (more men of University calibre are needed); the most modern equipment is required if they are to even hold their own in the fight against crime.

The Home Secretary recently promised increased efficiency in this battle against the crime wave. More use of modern aids such as two-way wireless sets—transistorised—would make the average constable on the beat more flexible; improvements in forensic aids to detection were also promised. A major research programme has just been started to identify, by automatic means, a single fingerprint left at the scene of the crime. Even the Atomic Research Establishment at Aldermaston has been brought into this project. There has been talk recently of the compulsory fingerprinting of everyone and this would obviously make the detection of crimes easier, although it would be an unpopular move with the ordinary citizen who would look upon it as an infringement of his personal liberty. Other means to easier detection could be expanded and elaborated. In 1927 Dr Crippen, the notorious murderer, was unfortunate enough to be caught by means of the first ever radio message sent to a ship by the police. Since then has enough use been made of modern communications? Appeals to the public through the media of the National Press, radio and television have yielded good results in the past and more use of this aid to detection is likely. Liverpool police now watch certain main streets from a control room by means of strategically placed television cameras—an expansion of this type of man-saving device is obviously a future certainty—we shall also see an increase in the use of identikits, requests for information by police on television and radio. The police will also become more mobile to counter the increased mobility of the criminal. It will not be long before policemen will regularly use helicopters in their everyday routine. Perhaps too we shall see an increase in the specialist squads of plain clothes detectives (C.I.D.) to combat the specialisation of criminals, e.g. fraud squads, narcotic squads.

In the meantime recruitment should be stepped up, for the most crowded urban areas where most of the criminals hide out are where the police are understrength. In Birmingham they are 25 per cent undermanned; much the same is true for London. (Policewomen (started in 1917) number about 2,000 and they also are too few in number.) Though the overall strength of the police is 83,000, it seems that not an economic enough use is made of it. The recommendations of the 1960–62 Royal Commission that far more of the smaller forces should amalgamate is being put into effect too slowly. In this, as in regional crime squads, faster reorganisation is imperative. Perhaps a national, centrally-controlled police force might be the best way of dealing with organised crime in the future. There will most probably be opposition to this, just as there was with the introduction of Henry Fielding's 'People', and the 'Peelers', but it is doubtful whether the cries of 'Cromwellism!' and 'Sidmouth's Spies!' will be heard, as they have been in the past.

Punishment If it is hard to pin down the reasons why crimes are committed, it is just as difficult to determine the most effective punishment for those caught and convicted. The question of what punishment wrong-doers should receive is the one most likely to arouse arguments, sometimes furious and often emotional. Each society has inflicted the punishment it thought was warranted; sometimes an attempt has been made to make the punishment fit the crime. In the Middle Ages serious crimes were punished by mutilations—a twice-caught thief might have his hands cut off. The traditional controversy has nearly always, however, revolved around the deterrent effect of punishment. Advocates of harsh penalties such as the 'cat' and the 'birch' sometimes adopt an Old Testament 'eye for an eye, tooth for a tooth' attitude to justice. Today there are several societies urging a return to well-tried severe punishments. But they are going against the trend of current thought. Since 1962 there has been no case of a prisoner being birched as a form of punishment— each individual birching has to be sanctioned by the Home Secretary.

End of Capital Punishment? The most hard-worked for, debated and controversial penal bill of the century came into force in November 1965. For a trial period of five years capital punishment was to be suspended. Already this measure is under attack and it will only need a marginal increase in the number of murders committed over the next few years for this progressive measure to be thrown out. Perhaps a national plebiscite would reveal a majority in favour of capital punishment and even corporal punishment but an increasing number of people believe that all types of severe punishment are useless. The criminal tends to be hardened and returned to society with even less chance of leading a lawful life than before. They advocate an extension of the more constructive methods such as probation and reformation, methods employed with reasonable success on juvenile delinquents and even adults. This philosophy of punishment is not far removed from that put out by George Bernard Shaw: 'To punish is to injure; to reform is to heal. You cannot mend a person by damaging him.'

The 'get-tougher-with-the-criminal' brigade are horrified that some men should actually prefer to be in prison rather than in society at large—they maintain that if their sentence were made more unpleasant they would try harder to lead a useful life outside. The fact is, however, that the worth of terror in the prevention of crime is not borne out by the history of the penal system. If this were so, then one would expect that the severer the punishments the fewer the crimes. The early nineteenth century penal system refutes this; when there were over 200 capital offences on the statute book crime continued unabated, yet when most were abolished there was no corresponding increase in offences. Even Peel, who holds an honoured place in the history of penal reform, regarded it as 'a most dangerous experiment' when stealing £5 from a dwelling house ceased to be a capital offence. After the gallows were largely replaced by the prisons the current philosophy was that convicts should endure a life as harsh and humiliating as possible. This, in turn, failed to deter and a committee set up to investigate the work of the prisons found that they were breeding grounds of crime and that the inmates were brutalised and demoralised. Oscar Wilde in *The Ballad of Reading Gaol*, in moving poetry, describes the degradation which prisoners experienced in the late nineteenth century. One of the points often forgotten by those who advocate severe punishments is that many

58 *The police dog.* Dogs such as Alsatians were used during the Second World War to guard camps and prisons, especially in Germany. Today they provide valuable assistance to the police when suspects are being chased.

crimes are committed on impulse and that the majority of criminals are too immature to visualise the results of their actions—to many of them the deterrent has no force at all and to others there may seem little chance of detection.

There will always be a criminal element in society made up largely of people who transgress the laws wittingly and for their own ends. The numbers may, perhaps, be kept to a minimum by catching the criminal young, before he is beyond reform as so many of the older ones are. This sphere of penal reform is the one most likely to expand in the future. Whether it comes from the growth of welfare services, the greater use of probation officers and psychologists, better schooling and careers' guidance (finding the job which suits) is uncertain. What is certain is that society has changed its attitude to offenders against the law. In the Middle Ages, mutilations and outlawry were the immediate retributions; penalties were designed not only to inflict pain but also to degrade and humiliate the offender, e.g. the stocks, ducking-stool and the pillory. The seventeenth and eighteenth centuries witnessed the system of hangings and transportation as the most common form of punishment, but today, although there are over 30,000 people lodged in prisons, more than twice that number are on probation. To abolish prison as a major form of punishment would be utopian; certain members have to be segregated from the rest of society.

There are schemes in progress, however, to rationalise the whole system of dealing with offenders. The probation service is being surveyed by a team of experts at the Home Office Research unit in an attempt to find out what kinds of treatment are the most effective. A detailed study of a sample of 700 male probationers aged seventeen to twenty-one is being made. If successful, the survey will prove an additional scientific guide both for magistrates and probation officers when the question of treatment arises for a particular type of offender. In addition to the probation survey it is likely that the whole system of imprisonment will be changed in the near future. The Home Office has recently outlined proposals to substitute for prison sentences a system of treatment in freedom. Major changes envisaged include institutions for the treatment of drug addicts and drunks (5,000 drunks are at present sent to prison every year); treatment other than prison for the 20,000

59 *Mail bags being sewn under maximum security.* An officer stands by as mailbags are sewn in the workroom of the new maximum security wing at Durham Gaol where the Great Train Robbers were detained before transference to the Isle of Wight.

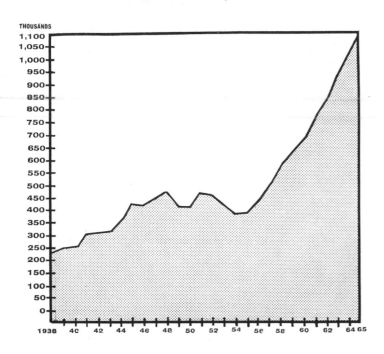

	Under 14		14–17		17–21		21–30		30 and over		Total		Total
	M	F	M	F	M	F	M	F	M	F	M	F	
1938 . .	14,724	835	11,645	912	10,131	1,320	14,321	2,071	17,858	4,646	68,679	9,784	78,463
1957 . .	23,697	1,580	18,149	1,681	16,962	2,059	24,964	2,498	32,156	7,174	115,928	14,992	130,920
1958 . .	26,050	2,033	21,628	2,064	21,322	2,461	27,499	2,975	32,835	7,847	129,334	17,380	146,714
1959 . .	25,869	1,968	23,059	2,287	22,342	2,238	30,086	2,933	34,378	8,030	135,734	17,456	153,190
1960 . .	27,622	2,319	24,749	2,670	25,068	2,703	32,144	3,309	34,282	8,616	143,865	19,617	163,482
1961 . .	29,890	2,845	28,244	3,305	27,667	3,193	35,770	3,930	37,146	10,227	158,717	23,500	182,217
1962 . .	28,922	2,967	30,569	3,764	31,864	3,489	41,500	4,716	43,212	12,772	176,067	27,708	203,775
1963 . .	27,477	2,699	33,663	3,945	34,271	3,547	43,719	4,981	44,981	12,435	184,111	27,607	211,718
1964 . .	22,786	2,725	32,796	4,506	35,750	3,910	42,738	4,960	42,405	12,686	176,475	28,787	205,262
1965 . .	22,376	2,697	32,818	4,979	40,486	4,318	47,099	5,275	44,645	13,742	187,424	31,011	218,435

60 Indictable offences 1938-65. The graph shows all the offences known to the police, the table the number of convictions for these offences. From the discrepancy between the total figures it can be seen that only one in five people are actually charged and found guilty.

fine and debt defaulters annually committed, substantial reduction in the 30,000 remands before conviction, 14,000 of whom are not sent to prison even when convicted; suspended sentences for the 5,000 first offenders imprisoned every year without the option of a fine; earlier release for suitable prisoners when one-third of their sentence has been served.

These measures would reduce the prison population by about 15 per cent and besides saving the tax-payers money would give prisons the space and time to make improvements which are long overdue. The most important measure in the long run is the proposal to allocate centres where assessments could be made of each type of prisoner and the type of treatment needed—then the small number needing

93

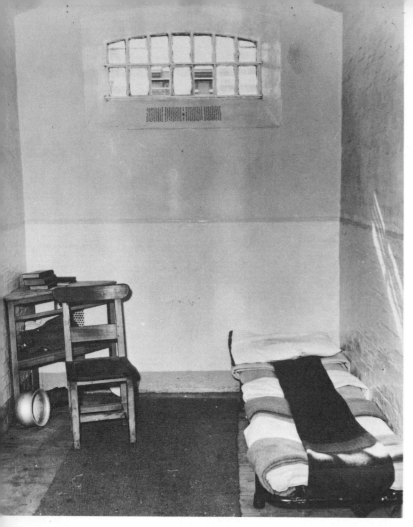

61 A cell inside Wormwood Scrubs. This cell is typical of most of those in the gaols of Britain today. The basic problem of modern prisons is how to combine treatment with security, and how to convert the nineteenth-century layout into an environment where human beings can live. Scandinavia and some American states, lead the way in modern prison layouts and practice, but Britain compares favourably with most other countries.

confinement under maximum security could be separated from the majority who did not. In the words of Lord Stonham (Joint Parliamentary Under Secretary, Home Office), 'It is a sad commentary on our own social development that we continue to immure them under a tightly disciplined regime, which is unnecessarily costly to the community and progressively harmful to the inadequate inmates.'

Reforms called for in previous centuries by John Howard and Elizabeth Fry are still being echoed today. It would be a pity if the efforts of these early pioneers were forgotten.

Further Reading   James Derriman, *Discovering the Law* (University of London Press 1962)
John Dedham, *A Young Man's Guide to the Law* (Hamish Hamilton 1965)
Arthur Groom, *How Law is Kept* (R.K.P. 1964)
F. T. Giles, *Children and the Law* (Penguin Books 1959)
J. Boswell Taylor, *999 Police* (University of London Press 1964)

The numbers in **bold type** refer to the numbers of the illustrations

Alderman, 9
Alexander the Great administers justice, **2**
Alfred the Great, 7
Anarchists, 80
Anglo-Saxon law, 7ff., 12, 116; **3, 4**
Askewe, Anne, burning of, **10**
Assize of Clarendon, 10
of Northampton (1178), 11
Australia, 64

Bambridge, Thomas, 64
Bank of England, 40
'Basket Justice', 26
Bedford, 16
Beggars, *see* Vagabonds
Benefit of Clergy, 14
Bentham, Jeremy, 46, 74
Berwick Borough Gaol, 66
Birmingham, 30, 32, 71, 76
Crime Research Unit, 86
Black Death, 31
'Blood Feast', 38
Boiling, death by, 23
Boke of Justyces of Peas, 20
Borough Police Forces, 78
Borsholder (Alderman), 9
Borstal, 72
Bot (compensation), 8
Bow Street, 41, 45, 59; **38**
Patrole (Mounted), 47, 49
Runners, 40, 42ff.; **25**
Brandeth, Jeremiah ('The Nottingham Captain'), 52, 53; **31**
Branding, 24
Braxfield, Judge, 64
Breaking on the wheel, 16
Bristol, 30
the burning of (1831); **35**
Brixton Prison, **46**
Burning, death by, 16, 22; **7, 10**
Buxton, Thomas E., 66

Cambridge Crime Research Unit, 86
Capital punishment, *see* Boiling, Burning, Executions, Hanging
end of, 90
Catholic martyrdom, **14**
Relief Bill (1778), 40
Cato Street Conspiracy, 56; **33**
Chancery, Court of, 18
Charles II, 27
'Charlies' (night-watchmen), 27, 47; **16, 21, 36**
Chartists, 75; **48**
Churchill, Mr Winston, 80; **53**
City Life, 32
Civil Law, 5
Cobbett, William, *Register*, **56**
Cock-fighting, 27
Colquhoun, Patrick, 46, 47, 49, 57
Combination Acts (1799), 45

Common Law, 6, 29
Pleas, Court of, 18
Compurgation, 13
Conservators of the Peace, 12
Constables, 12, 34, 40, 49
Corn Laws, 50
Corrective Training, 73
Corruption, 19, 21, 36
Court Leet, 10
'Crank, the', 71, 72
Crime, causes and increase of, 86
prevention, 89
Criminal Justice Act (1948), 72
Law, 5
Cromwellian period, justice during, 26
Curia Regis, 9, 10, 18

Dark Ages, the, 7
Death Penalty, *see* Capital Punishment
Debtors' prisons, 47
Defoe, Daniel, 29, 30, 34
Derbyshire Rising (1817), 52
Detective force, the first separate, 78
Dickens, Charles, 21, 57
Disraeli, Benjamin, 50
Ducking punishment, **18**
Duelling, 27; **34**
Durham Gaol, **59**

Ecclesiastical Law, 6
Education Act (1870), 78
Edward the Confessor, 9
Edward I, King, 10, 11, 13
III, 12
IV, 17
Embracery, 16
Enclosure, effects of, 31ff.
Exchequer, Court of the, 18
Executions, 16, 37, 56, 62, 69; **7, 8, 10, 17, 22, 28, 44**

Fanhope, Lord, 16
Farm labourers, 32
Fenian Revolt, 29, 80
Fielding, Henry and John, 33, 34, 37, 41; **24**
Enquiry into the Cause of Robberies, 42
Fingerprinting, compulsory, 89
Fleet Prison, 40, 44, 64
Flogging, 65, 68; **42**
Ford, Richard (magistrate), 46
French Revolution, 40
Fry, Elizabeth, 57, 64, 65, 67, 74; **43**

Game Laws, 50; **30**
George I, 30
II, 30, 32, 40

Gin Acts (1736 and 1751), 34
drinking, 34; **20**
Gladstone, Herbert, 72
Golding, William, *Lord of the Flies*, 5
Good, Daniel (murderer), 78
Gordon, Lord George, and Gordon Riots, 40, 44; **27**
Great Train Robbery, 88; **59**
Grenville, George, 46
Gresham, Manor of, 16
Greville, Charles, 77
Gurney, John and Elizabeth, 66

Habeas Corpus Act (1679), 29, 45
Hanging, 37, 62, 68; **22, 28, 44**
end of, 90
Hanging, drawing and quartering, 16, 22
Harold, King, 9
Henry I, 9
II, 9, 10
VII, 17, 19, 24
VIII, 21, 22, 28
Hitchcock, Richard, 24
Hogarth, 34
Gin Lane (print), **20**
Home Secretary, 38, 52, 56, 58, 92
Houses of Correction, 24, 66
Howard, John, 57, 64, 74
State of Prisons (1777), 64
Howard League for Penal Reform, 73
Huddersfield, 51
Hue and Cry, 12
Hulks, Prison, 64
Hundreds (administrative districts), 8
Hunt, 'Orator', 52, 54, 55

Identikit, **57**
Improvement Acts and Commissioners, 30
Industrial Revolution, 40

Jacels, burning of, **10**
Jacobite Risings (1715 and 1745), 39
James I, King, 26
John, King, 10, 11
Johnson, Dr Samuel, 34
Jury, majority verdict, 88
Justices of the Peace, 12, 18, 20, 21, 30, 36, 53
corruption among, 36

King's Court (Witan), 7; **1**
Peace, 8, 9, 10
Kinship in Anglo-Saxon Law, 8

Labour Party, 78
Liverpool, 30

Locke, John, 84
Lombard, William, 20
London, 23, 30, 33, 57
  low life in, 32–34; **19, 20**
Lord Lieutenants, 53
Lovett, William, 76
Luddite Riots, 51, 52, 53, 75

Mackintosh, Sir James, 57
Magistrates, 36, 40, 59
Magna Carta, 11, 29
Manchester, 30, 54, 55; **32**
Marine Police headquarters established (1798), 46
Marx, Karl, 50, 74
Metropolitan Police, 56, 59, 74; **38, 49–51**
  See also Bow Street Runners
Militia to maintain order, use of, 26, 50, 52–54, 79, 81
Mob, the, 30, 32, 44; **26**
  See also Riots
Mohocks, 28
Moleyns, Lord, 16

Newcastle, Riots in (1740), 33
Newgate Prison, 40, 44, 63, 65; **23, 42**
Newport, Chartist Riots at, 48
Night watchmen, *see* 'Charlies'
Norman Conquest, 8, 9
  influence, 9ff.
Norwich, 23
Nottingham Assizes (1812), 51

Oath helpers, 12
Oath, taking the, **3**
O'Connor, Feargus, 76
Oglethorpe, 64
Oldham, 30
Oliver the Spy, 52, 53
Ordinance for the Reform of Manners (1654), 27
Owen, Robert, 76

Palmer, Execution of Dr, **44**
Pankhurst, Mrs, 81
Parish constables, 34, 49
Peel, Sir Robert, 49ff., 56ff., 74; **37**
'Peelers, The', 59; **38, 49–51**
Penal System, the present, 84
Pentonville Prison, 67, 71; **45**
'Peterloo, Massacre of', 54, 55; **32**
Philadelphia State Penitentiary, 67
Pillory, 15; **6, 29**
Pitt, William, 45, 46, 50
Platter, Thomas, *Travels in England*, 62
Poaching, 50; **30**
Pocket-picking removed from list of capital offences, 57
Police, 40, 53, 59, 74, 78; **38, 49–51, 55–57**

Act, 89
bulletin, first, 44
dogs, **58**
public antipathy to the idea of, 52, 59
Rate levied, 59
Policewomen, 90; **56**
Poor, the problem of the 23ff., 32, 44, 50
Poor Law, 24
Population increase, 30
Preston House of Correction, 66
Preventive detention, 73
Prison, 14, Chap. 6; **42, 43, 45–47, 60, 61**
  corruption in management of, 64
  maximum security, **59**
  reform, 57, 64
Prisons Acts (1791, 1835), 63, 65
Probation of Offenders Act (1908), 72
Probation Service, 92
Public Hue and Cry, 44
Punishments,
  Medieval, 14, 16; **5, 6, 7**
  Tudor, 22; **10–12, 14, 15**
  18th century, 37; **18, 23**
  19th century, 47ff., 56, 57, 62ff.; **28, 29, 39–45**
  20th century, 90; **59–61**

Quarter Sessions, 12
Quarterly Pursuit, 44

Ratcliffe Highway Murders (1811), 47
Reform Bills, 74–76
  League, 79
Regency 'Bucks', **36**
Richard I, King, 12
Riot Act (1715), 40
Riots, 40, 44, 50–52, 60, 61, 75, 76; **26, 27, 35**
River Police, 46
Romilly, Sir Samuel, 57, 64, 74
Ruthven (Bow Street Runner), 43

St George's Fields Massacre (1768), 44
Sanctuary, 14
Sayer (Bow Street Runner), 43, 48
Sheriffs, 10
Shires, 8
Shop detectives, 88
Sidmouth, Lord (Home Secretary), 52, 53, 55, 56
Siege of Sidney Street, 80; **53**
Six Acts, The (1819), 54, 55
Slavery, 24
Social Distress, Victorian, 76
Spa Fields Meeting (1816), 54
Special Branch, 80
  Constables, **52**
Star Chamber, 20, 28
Statute Law, 6

Statute of Westminster, 11, 18, 30
Stocks, 15; **5**
Strikes, 81, 83
Stuart Law, 26ff.; **16**
Stubbes' *Anatomie of Abuses*, 62
Suffragettes, 81; **54**

Thames Police Bill (1800), 46
Thanes, 9
Thistlewood, Arthur, 56
Tithings, 9
Torture, 13, 16; **15**
Townshend, 'Turnip', 32
Townshend (Bow Street Runner), 48; **25**
Townships (vills), 8
Trade Unionism, 76, 81
Transportation, 37, 64; **39, 40**
Treadwheel, 66, 68, 72
Treason, 16
Trial by jury, 13, 88
  by ordeal, 12; **4**
Tudor Justice, 18ff.; **10–13**
Tull, Jethro, 32

Underworld, Elizabethan, 21; **9**
  slang, 22
Unemployment, 21ff., 26, 30, 32, 40, 50, 54; **52**
Urbanisation, increase of, 30

Vagabonds, 21–23, 24, 30, 32; **11, 12**
Van Diemens Island, 64; **40**
Vaughan, George (Bow Street Runner), 48
Veil, Colonel de, 41
Vickaray (Bow Street Runner), 43
Victorian Era, 74ff.

Wakefield Prison, 65, 71
Walpole's Excise Scheme (1733), 39
Wapentakes, 8
Wards and Liveries, Court of, **13**
Watch and Ward, 12, 18, 30, 53
Watchmen, *see* 'Charlies'
Water torture, **15**
Weekly Pursuit, 44
Wellington, Duke of, 50, 56
Wergild, 8, 15
Wilberforce, William, 64
Wild, Jonathan, 37, 41; **22**
Wilkes, John, 32, 40, 44; **26**
William the Conqueror, 9, 14
Williams, John (murderer), 47
Witan, 7, 9; **1**
Women convicts, 66, 68; **43, 46**
Wormwood Scrubs, **60, 61**
Wright, Sampson, 45
Wrongus Imprisonment Act (1701), 29

Young, Arthur, 33